INDY
THE WORLD'S FASTEST CARNIVAL RIDE

THE WORLD'S FASTEST CARNIVAL RIDE

by Dan Gerber
with photos by Heinz Kluetmeier

PRENTICE-HALL, INC., Englewood Cliffs, New Jersey

Also by Dan Gerber

Novels
AMERICAN ATLAS
OUT OF CONTROL

Poems
THE REVERANT
DEPARTURE

INDY/THE WORLD'S FASTEST CARNIVAL RIDE
by Dan Gerber
Copyright © 1977 by Dan Gerber
Photos © 1977 by Heinz Kluetmeier
A portion originally appeared in the June 1976 issue of *Playboy* Magazine

Book Design by Hal Siegel and Linda Huber
Art Direction by Hal Siegel

Printed in the United States of America
Prentice-Hall International, Inc., London
Prentice-Hall of Australia, Pty. Ltd., Sydney
Prentice-Hall of Canada, Ltd., Toronto
Prentice-Hall of India Private Ltd., New Delhi
Prentice-Hall of Japan, Inc., Tokyo
Prentice-Hall of Southeast Asia Pte. Ltd., Singapore
Whitehall Books Limited, Wellington, New Zealand

10 9 8 7 6 5 4 3 2 1

Library of Congress Cataloging in Publication Data
Gerber, Daniel F
  Indy, the world's fastest carnival ride.

  1. Indianapolis Speedway Race. I. Title.
GV1033.5.I55G47   796.7'2'0680977252   76-28812
ISBN 0-13-464156-6

**Half Title photo: Spike Gehlhausen, the youngest
rookie in the field, goes out for practice**

Title page photo: A. J. Foyt

This book is for Robert F. Jones

Preface

As God created man and woman, so too He fashioned the hero and the poet, or orator. The poet cannot do what the other does; he can only admire, love and rejoice in the hero. Yet he too is happy, and not less so, for the hero is as it were his better Nature, with which he is in love.

Johannes de Silento

When someone discovers that I am a writer, the first question usually asked is, "What do you write about?" I've never really known how to answer that, though it occurs to me now that the only really frank response is: "I write about me; that is, I write about me in the context of a given experience." It doesn't matter whether it's an actual physical experience or a purely imaginative one. I'm the only subject I feel competent to deal with. I might take the form of a poem or a novel or, as in the case of this book, an auto race-circus-ritual migration-jousting tournament-nightmare-extravaganza-religious pilgrimage: the most truly American celebration of the arrival of summer.

The Indianapolis Motor Speedway is a two-and-one-half-mile oval, fifty feet wide on the straightaways and sixty feet wide on each of its four idiosyncratic turns. When it was built by a group of Indianapolis sportsmen in 1909 as a place to test their new toy, the automobile, it was a dirt track. Later it was paved with bricks and finally with asphalt, but its width, banking and configuration have not been altered since the cars that raced on it were incapable of averaging more than eighty miles an hour. Except

for the years of the Second World War, a five-hundred-mile race
has been run on it every Memorial Day weekend since 1911. It
has become the single most important and most prestigious
automobile race, is broadcast over seven hundred domestic and
five hundred foreign radio stations, is witnessed on television by
an estimated 22 million people and draws more spectators than
any other sporting event in the world. Hundreds of millions of
dollars have been spent by those who have tried to win it, and in
its sixty-year history, it has taken fifty-three lives.

Heinz Kluetmeier had covered the Indianapolis 500 for *Sports
Illustrated* since 1971. When I talked to him about the idea of this
book, he seemed as enthusiastic about it as I was. We agreed
it would require another month in Indianapolis to bear down on
the experience. So in 1976 we went back for the month of May,
not for *Sports Illustrated* or for *Playboy*, as I had done the year
before, but for ourselves.

What we came back with were two experiences spanning
four years in and around the Speedway. The photographs were
not taken to illustrate the text. They simply record Heinz's vision
graphically as I have recorded mine in words. Later we selected
almost two hundred photographs from the more than ten thousand,
accumulated both for their intrinsic qualities and to the degree
that our experience coincided, to complement what I had written.

We have both been alternately fascinated, repelled,
enthralled, horrified, titillated, exhausted and stunned by the event
—not just the race itself, but all the energy surrounding it that
boils over into beauty, craziness, death, desperation, sloth,
Babbittry, courage and a drama in which the drivers are merely the
main characters in a pageant that wouldn't work without a
supporting cast of thousands—no, of hundreds of thousands.

D. G.

In the early fifties it was a movie starring Clark Gable, titled *To Please a Lady*, with actual race footage and the faces of real drivers like Mauri Rose and Wilbur Shaw and huge ferocious cars resembling U-boats on wheels.

The tires were absurdly narrow and grooved with tread only on the right half of the running surface. The movie was my first glimpse of a world that had previously enthralled me purely with sound. I was ten years old and had already decided that to become a racing driver and to drive at Indianapolis was the only thing worth growing up for. Each Memorial Day was spent with engine sounds and the voice of Sid Collins. It didn't matter much what he said; it was just the sound of his voice switching to his reporters around the track, the roar of the cars in the background and the litany of what were, for me, almost holy names: Troy Ruttman, Tony Bettenhausen, Jimmy Bryan, Sam Hanks, Johnnie Parsons, Pat O'Connor and, most holy of all, Billy Vukovich. It meant school was getting out and I could get sunburned and go fishing and spend three months on Lake Michigan trying to let the magic names fade into some kind of perspective. Whenever I wasn't in a bathing suit I wore slightly grimy white duck trousers and a grease-smudged white T-shirt, because that's what "Vuky" had been wearing in the one photo I'd seen of him, sitting on a workbench, barefooted, his knees pulled up to his chest, exhausted and dejected after leading the 1952 race for 191 laps until a fifty-cent steering part let go and put him into the northeast wall. "The tough little driver from Fresno," the papers called him, using his standard quote, "Just don't get in my way."

Then Vuky won in 1953 and again in '54. It was the way it had to be. Speeds had climbed past the 140-mph barrier and everybody wondered if they hadn't reached the limit. "We're going too fast out there," Vuky said. "Well Vuky, " the interviewer reflected, "you're the only one who can slow it down." But he didn't slow it down. He qualified for the 1955 race at 141.071 mph, led the race for 56 laps, then crashed and was killed attempting to avoid a pileup on the back straight. I saw the newsreel and the photograph of the now-primitive-looking Hopkins Special lying upside down, the hand of my boyhood hero protruding from the cockpit as if waving good-by. I remember feeling somehow responsible for Vuky's death. It was the first time I hadn't listened to the race. My father had taken me fishing in Ontario, and on Memorial Day we were flying down from Saddle Lake in a pontoon plane when the bush pilot tuned in the race on his radio and told us that Vukovich had been killed. I asked him to turn it off. I didn't want to hear the cars or Sid Collins and the magic names if Vuky wasn't among them anymore.

Another year went by and my aversion to racing cooled. But it would never be quite the same without Vuky. My interest turned to roadracing and more exotic, if somehow less personally awesome names, like Juan Fangio, Stirling Moss, Phil Hill and the Marquis de Portago. It was more intricate and interesting racing, and I learned to pronounce Le Mans like the French, and Sebring

◀ The last yard of bricks on the start-finish line, preserved when the brick track was paved over in 1963 and the Mille Miglia and Nurburgring. But as much as I pontificated that it was dumb to turn left all the time, Indy and Sid Collins and Tony Hulman orating "Gentlemen, start your engines," was still where the magic was.

The day I got my driver's license I borrowed, without permission, a 1955 Thunderbird and pushed the speedometer needle up over 100 to see what it felt like to *be* Vuky; speed is always in the present tense. I raced motorcycles and an assortment of cars and pickup trucks on Michigan back roads, and two weeks after my twenty-first birthday, drove my first real race on a dirt track in an Austin Healy, and won. A boyhood friend who, with skepticism and boredom, had endured years of my racing dreams, now regarded me with a certain reverence and said, "Well, Vuky, you really did it." It was a farfetched comparison, but at that moment I was God's gift to racing and Indianapolis seemed only a short step away.

I never drove at Indianapolis. I never even came close. I raced sports cars for five years, with moderate success, then stuffed one into the end of the pit wall at Riverside, broke every bone in my body and quit. For seven years I stayed away from racing, not wishing to taunt myself with failed aspirations. Then, two years ago at the invitation of Bob Jones, a friend who covers racing for *Sports Illustrated*, I went to Indianapolis to watch qualifying and the race. Somehow I always knew that sooner or later I'd have to confront this track, if not as a driver then at least as a spectator.

It wasn't quite the way it had been in *To Please a Lady*. The bricks had been covered with asphalt, the great wooden pagoda replaced by a glass and steel tower and most of the names had changed. There was a Bettenhausen, a Parsons and a Vukovich; and though they were a new generation of drivers, the sons of the men I had idolized, the names retained their fascination. There were newer names that had acquired their own aura—Foyt, Ruby, Unser and Andretti—and several, like Donahue and Revson, I'd competed with on road courses ten years earlier. I remember being a little awed by the realization that those men I'd learned to race with, and sometimes beaten, were driving and even winning at Indianapolis. Of course they weren't the same men, and neither was I. But Indianapolis was the same track (at least it was in the same place) and coming to it finally was like visiting a historic battleground, with one important exception. Another battle would soon be fought here and another and another. New monuments would be built over the old. Racing drivers must perforce live totally in the present and pay no more than a token deference to last year's winner or last year's dead.

That was in 1973, and it proved a bad year to reacquaint myself with racing. During the final practice session before qualifying began, I had just come through the 16th Street tunnel on my way to the pits when I heard a loud *wuump* and turned to see Art Pollard's car, both right wheels broken off on impact with the wall, sliding sideways through the short chute. About one hundred feet in front of me, the axle stubs dug into the infield grass and the car began flipping. Upside down, it skidded back onto the track, flipped right side up and came to rest in the middle of turn two. Pollard sat motionless amid the alcohol flames, visible only as heat vapors rising from the car, and at that moment,

a strange thing happened. Looking back on it, it seems improbable, but I could have sworn I heard the crowd in the bleachers on the far side of the track, in unison, scream, "Save him!"

It was a full thirty seconds before the crash truck arrived, put out the flames and extracted Pollard from the car. The two disembodied wheels rolled together in formation and came to rest in the infield as neatly as if they'd been stacked there for future use. Several hours later, in an interval between qualification attempts, they announced that Pollard was dead. A fat woman in the bleachers behind the pits broke into tears. There was an official minute of silence, then qualifying resumed. The announcer announced a new one-lap record. The fat lady was cheering.

Two weeks later I came back, waited through the tension of two days of race-delaying rain and two aborted starts, one of them catastrophic, and went home. I watched the carnage on television, Salt Walther's legs protruding from the wreckage of his burning, spinning car, Swede Savage's fatal crash in turn four and the STP crewman hit and killed by an emergency truck speeding to the rescue. It seemed a more macabre spectacle couldn't have been planned. Indy had lived up to its reputation and anyone who'd paid his five dollars hoping he might see blood got his money's worth.

The rules were changed in the interests of safety. The fuel capacity of the car was halved to diminish fire hazard. The size of the airfoils was cut, and pop-off valves installed on the turbochargers to limit boost, all in hopes of slowing the cars down. The track facility was improved, spectator barriers strengthened, the pit entrance widened and the inside wall in turn four, the one that had killed Savage, eliminated. The 1974 race was one of the safest in the Speedway's history, no fatalities and no serious injuries. *Maybe I would go back to Indianapolis*, I thought. After all, it's the possibility of an accident that is racing's fascination, the risk, without which racing would be sterile and pointless; but it's the almost historical certainty that sometime during the month of May, someone would be killed there that has tended to make Indy seem more like a Roman circus than a twentieth-century sporting event.

May 2, 1975. The day before the track opens and I've got nothing to do but pick up my credentials and have a look around. It's quiet, almost eerie, like visiting an amusement park closed for the winter. Nothing seems to be moving and the only sound is the grandstand-muffled traffic passing on Sixteenth Street. Two men are painting new Coca-Cola and Sprite billboards on the scoring tower at the north end of the infield. In Gasoline Alley a dilapidated golf cart sits outside locked garage doors near the pit entrance, Jim Hurtubise–#56–Miller High Life, in oxidized red letters. It has two flat tires and looks as if it hasn't been touched since the previous May. Strange to think of this huge arena empty all but one month a year. The seasons change, the pits, the track and the grandstands covered with snow, but in everyone's mind—everyone but a few maintenance men and administrators—this place has no existence apart from the month of May, and to those for whom racing is a way of life, it *is* the month of May. I stand in the middle of the front straight where, the next day, highly specialized machines would be traveling at over 220 miles an hour. Heat waves rise from the track and the huge tier of grandstands above turn four. Now there's one sound, a regularly sequenced rachidic burst. I walk back into Gasoline Alley and around the rows of ancient wooden garages till I find its source, a mechanic with bulletproof thick bifocals, an oil-soaked cowboy hat and a patch on the back of his shirt that says: *Smokey's—Best Damm Garage in Town*. He's sitting on what looks like a railway baggage cart, polishing the ports of an intake manifold with an air-powered buffer, the first indication that someone's got in mind to go racing here.

To kill time, I take the fifty-cent track tour in a Chevrolet minibus. Once around the Speedway while the driver, with marginal accuracy, relays the speed the racers would be traveling, swings the van high on the nine-degree banking to show us how close the cars come to the wall, points out the prices of various grandstand and tower terrace seats and the locations of the most recent notable crashes: "Salt Walther ended up here, and he'll be racing again this year. Swede Savage hit the wall right there where there used to be a wall, and the part of the car with him in it ended up way down here." I find myself silently augmenting his list with the names of heroes and friends: Pollard in the south chute, Pat O'Connor in turn two, Vukovich on the back straight, Jim Malloy in turn three, Eddie Sachs and Dave MacDonald in turn four—their names now eclipsed by Swede Savages's.

At first reflection, this catalog of crash locations—both the minibus driver's and my own—seems a morbid preoccupation with tragedy, but these are places of history (like the location of Pickett's charge at Gettysburg or the box at Ford's Theatre in Washington), important to us for the violently abbreviated lives with which we have identified our own. What seems morbid to me is the propensity of most racing people and sports journalists to pretend those deaths never occurred. I remember that I was fishing in Key West with Bob Jones when we heard the news that Peter Revson had been killed practicing for the South African Grand Prix. I had known Revson and raced against him back in the early sixties. Jones had done a personality piece on Revson for *Sports Illustrated* and spent many evenings with him in the course of five years covering major races. The news came over the radio, and for what seemed like almost an hour, neither of us had anything to say. Finally, when so much time had elapsed that it seemed to come almost out of context, Jones said, "You realize that for the next six months now, nobody will mention his name."

"Yeah," I reflected, "and when they do it'll be as if he had lived twenty years ago."

It is easy to understand this sense of detachment among the drivers. If they were to ponder too deeply the dangers to themselves or the deaths of their competitors, their imaginations would take control and make it impossible for them to continue. Physical courage relies, to a great extent, on the ability to suspend

The Speedway Museum

Former winners in the Speedway Museum

Waiting in line to take track tour

the imagination, and sometimes this kind of control is transmitted to the outsider as callousness. I was standing a few feet away when Johnny Rutherford was interviewed shortly after the death of his close friend Art Pollard. "It's too bad that you can't turn back the clock," he said matter-of-factly. "Art was doing what he loved to do, and there's a risk we all take." His statement seemed to echo Faulkner's that "The irrevocability of action is tragic." A few minutes later, Rutherford went back out on the track, qualified for the pole and set a new one-lap record of 199.071 mph, a heroic effort that would have been impossible for any man whose mind hadn't been totally on his business.

The tour bus pauses in front of the pits and the driver explains how the names of the drivers qualifying for the race will be painted: "Right between them various red marks you see along that wall there." The teenage girl sitting next to me spots a driver with long frizzy hair and a flowered Hawaiian shirt. "There's Rick Muther. Hey Rick, Rick, can I have your autograph?" Muther is talking with another girl and seems not to hear the request.

Saturday, May 3, and the track is supposed to officially open for practice, but the sky is overcast and threatens rain. Nobody expects any really hot laps the first day out, and with qualifications still a week away, most of the top drivers haven't shown up. There are several rookies (highly experienced racers, but new to Indianapolis) who must learn the track and turn twenty observed laps within each of several speed brackets to pass their driver's test, and a few veterans, anxious to get back in the groove and check out their cars. The only real question on anyone's mind is, Who will be the first driver on the track? Being first out has no effect on qualifying or on the race but, like everything else here, is part of a tradition. It's supposed to be a coup. It generates a good deal of publicity, and publicity is what attracts sponsors and sells their products. It's why Gatorade and Surfine Foods and Jorgensen Steel invest up to three hundred thousand dollars to run this race, the hope that their sponsorship will generate millions of dollars worth of publicity, maybe even get a picture of their car, their billboard on wheels, on the cover of a national magazine, the kind of advertising money alone can't buy.

Dick Simon, a forty-one-year-old retired insurance executive from Salt Lake City, wheels his car to the end of the pit lane, ready to go. Then a few drops of rain fall and his crew covers the car with a plastic sheet. A band of Scottish pipers march onto the track and the absurdly elaborate pageantry of May in Indianapolis had begun. Every flower show, car wash and tea party will append the label, 500 Festival. Today's official events include a radio-controlled model-car race, a bridge tournament, a Dress Up Like Mom parade, a Look Like Your Favorite Television Personality contest, a bubble-gum blowing contest; and the mayor's breakfast at which 1,665 paying guests would hear Jimmy (the Greek) Snyder pick A. J. Foyt as the race winner, meet the 500 festival queen and then adjourn to the track for opening ceremonies, where each of those attending the breakfast would be permitted to make one lap of the track in their Corvette or Cadillac.

The thirty-three official Buick pace cars stream by bearing celebrities. I'm leaning on the pit fence, eavesdropping on two Speedway guards, sad-faced old men with the perennial look of

1957 race winner, Sam Hanks

small boys who got what they wanted for Christmas and then discovered it didn't make any difference. "Who was that boy got his head cut off down in Dayton? Shit, that 'as a good track till they ruined it with blacktop. You could come outta turn one, aim 'er at the grandstand, pour the coals to it and slide 'er all the way round. I remember when Mel Kenyon slid..." The Speedway, Indiana High School Band plays, "The Eyes of Texas," for Johnny Rutherford, last year's winner. A few more drops of rain. The festival queen accepts her crown and steps up to the microphone: "I wanna reckanize the twenty-eight princesses behind me." Now it's pouring. The band marches off, the crowd scatters for cover and Dick Simon's car sits abandoned, fogging its plastic shroud in the pit lane. The rain pools up all afternoon, discouraging everyone but the golfers on the Speedway golf course, their official black and white umbrellas dotting the fairways.

The bar at the Speedway Motel has the atmosphere of a neighborhood tavern. Everybody knows everybody, and if you don't know everybody, everybody knows you don't. But the waitress will flirt with you all the same and you're invited to listen in on any stories you like. It's fairly quiet this evening and as I sipped my gin and tonic I remembered sitting there the evening after Art Pollard's crash, overhearing a large man with ruptured capillaries tell how once in Korea he'd put a forty-five to the head of his "moose," when he'd come back to his "hooch," and found her "shackin up with a nigger supply sergeant."

"Whad you do?" his companion asked.

"I shot 'er head off."

"Really?"

"Yeh, but I missed and shot off her foot instead." The scalp beneath his silver flattop flared with laughter and, still laughing, he turned toward me. "Say, you don't know what happened to that fella crashed in turn one do ya?"

"He's dead." I didn't want to discuss Pollard in this context, but it was the only straight answer to his question.

"Aw shit, I'm sorry," he said, as if apologizing to me.

"You really shot her in the foot, huh?" His companion was intrigued.

"Naw, I never hit her at all. I just shot the bed full of holes." He leaned toward the bar and covered his face with his hand. "Aw Jesus," he said and began weeping. Something bumped my leg, and I noticed seat belts dangling from each of the bar stools.

It was getting dark and the rain still hadn't let up. A man well decorated with official badges and patches introduced himself. "Everybody knows everybody here."

"So I noticed."

"These paintings, see these paintings on the walls?" He swept his hand in a slow circle indicating a half-dozen pictures by Leroy Neiman, impressions of the 1963 race. "They're valued at more than a million dollars, and they don't even have a guard here to watch 'em. Like I said, everybody knows everybody here, and they're good people." I raised my glass and we drank to the good people. "I'm the weighmaster here."

"Pardon me?"

"I'm the weighmaster. I weigh the cars. My company's got twenty-five thousand invested in the scales, and we can't afford to have anything go wrong." I raised my glass again and we drank to his scales.

The next morning a rookie named Billy Scott beat Dick Simon to the track. Scott passed his driver's test with no problems. "A cakewalk," he said to me as he stepped out of his car. But Jigger Sirois, who in six years at the Speedway had yet to make the race, was having trouble again. He took four or five laps to warm his engine, then stood on it coming past the pits. I was standing next to a track photographer when we heard the engine noise fade in the first turn, the horrible scrubbing of tires, an instant of silence and the dull, grinding thud of rubber, steel and fiberglass embracing concrete. "Oh goddam Jigger"—the photographer slapped his thigh—"he done it again." Now the track was officially open. A middle-aged lady with ultramarine blue wings painted on her

eyelids. The wing tips extend to her temples. No cars are moving now, and she's leaning on the pit fence, casting a spell on the empty grandstands across the track. The infield bleachers are three-quarters full of spectators, yawning and turning pink. They respond like a chorus each time they hear the putter of a wheel horse or the pit-gate guard blow his whistle, stretching their spines to see whose car is being pushed into the pits, then collapsing again in the shade of their newspapers, swatting flies and occasionally each other. The guards drag off a streaker.

With the exception of the two qualifying weekends and the race itself, it'll go on this way most of the month. Already there is gossip about cheating, and Foyt, as everyone's nemesis, is the center of attention. George Bignotti, who for years had been Foyt's crew chief, had publicly accused Foyt of carrying more fuel than the rules allow. Foyt won the California 500 in a walkaway, and Bignotti had suggested he'd done it carrying an extra five gallons of methanol in the canister of his fire extinguisher. The controversy raged all month, and though the concerns were genuine, I sensed a certain patina of showmanship.

When and if he would finally get around to it no one, even those with the most peripheral interest in racing, seriously entertained the possibility that anyone could go faster than A. J. The hitchhikers I'd picked up the night before had no doubt about it.

"We come up here with a couple a cunts, but they dropped us." He was wearing the first honest-to-God duck's-ass hairdo I'd seen since 1961. "'Course we was drunk, I'll give 'em that. But you can bet your ass I'll be straddling my B.M.W. the next time I hit this town." He leaned forward from the backseat and tapped me on the shoulder. "Say, you an Elk?"

"No."

"You ain't even from around here, is you?" The one beside me had tattoos on his arms.

"No."

"Well if you was, you'd be an Elk too. We're from Greencastle. Ever hear of it?"

"Something about Dillinger. He robbed a bank there didn't he?"

"He sure did." The tattooed one seemed to point to it as a matter of civic pride. "Everybody knows that I guess."

The D.A. laid his arm across my shoulder and pointed to an overpass about a mile ahead. "You can just drop us off on my bridge up there."

"Your bridge?" I was being set up.

"I laid every inch of concrete in that sucker and sloped the banks with a dozer. I 'as the first one to drive across it too."

In the rearview mirror, I could see I was being regarded with suspicion, a foreigner, not even an Elk. "What're you doin here anyway?"

"I'm here for the race."

"Well I don't give much of a shit about that, but I know Foyt's got a few more miles in his pocket. You wait an' see."

"Can I quote you?"

"Hell, I said it didn't I?"

On the first day of qualifying, Foyt pulled in after one lap at
189.195. It was the fastest lap turned in during the first half hour
of qualifications, but not close to the 192 plus laps he'd been
turning in practice. He ranted around the pits, ostentatiously
complaining about his tires, then stormed off to his garage and
locked the doors. The story went around that he was so pissed off
he'd taken a screwdriver and punctured all four tires on his car.
"That'd be a good trick," he said later, "I'd like to see somebody
try it." There was also some speculation that the tire tantrum was
a ploy to get his car back into the garage so he could tamper with
the turbocharger pop-off valve installed by the United States Auto
Club (USAC) and illegally increase its pressure.

Late in the afternoon when the track was cooler and three
other cars had qualified at over 190, A. J. tried again. The first time
he went by, everyone knew that, if he survived, the pole position
would be his. I watch him power through turn two, using every
inch of the track. I can feel everyone around me holding his breath,
A. J.'s engine screaming at full power, watching him slide to the
backstraight wall till there isn't an inch of daylight between his

right rear tire and the unimpressionable concrete. I can feel his engine vibrate all the way down the back straight and into turn three. No one is really surprised when they announce his first lap speed of 195.313 mph, and we know we were watching something so frivolously momentous, so ethereally and courageously executed and yet so seemingly pointless: a man, unquestionably the best in the world at what he does, transcending even his own abilities, placing himself at the mercy of intricately overstressed steel and rubber and any stray speck of dirt on the track, to go nowhere faster than anyone else possibly could. For three minutes and five and a half seconds all the allegations of cheating seem pointless. A. J. Foyt owns the track and no one will dispute it. "I thrilled the hell outta myself three or four times out there," he says, just to let everyone know it hasn't been quite as easy or predetermined as it looks.

Apart from Foyt's run, the greatest spectator interest on the front straight is generated by a rabbit. Qualifying is stopped and several spectators chase the rabbit up and down the track in front of the pits, the crowd cheering, as in the lion feeding scenes from *Quo Vadis*, each time they pass. The rabbit has strayed into a jungle without cover, nothing but asphalt, concrete walls, and four pairs of Addidas track shoes pursuing him. Five minutes later he is strung from the infield fence, dead from an apparent heart attack.

A. J. Foyt getting ready for his qualifying run

In the bleachers behind the pit fence, I notice a cheering section of thirty or forty men in orange T-shirts. I'm attracted by the wry, subtle wit of the posters they've hung from the railing in front of their seats: *Fire Up Go Nuts, Super Tits, Take I-69 to the 500, Give Harlen the Fengler,* and *I'll Bet My Ass on Loydd's Rubys.* One sign, *Sandy Lovelace* [with a phone number], they disclaimed but admitted they'd rented the space to a new girl in town and that they'd "all been behind her 1,000 percent." Their P.R. man insists I have a Coors with him before he'll answer any questions. It's a hot day and I hadn't realized how thirsty I was. "You're okay," he tells me. "We like the way you drink your beer."

The Classics were founded by "fifteen men of like vision," in 1963 and have had the same block of seats each year since. They even have a special Speedway guard assigned to protect and contain them. "For years it was Pops Middleton, but when he died we acquired ole Larry here." The P.R. man put his arm around the porcine and obviously pleased track attendant who beamed deferentially from under his pith helmet. "We got our own hospitality suite at the Mayfair Motel and our own clubhouse here under the stands. That's where we have our Rookie of the Year Contest."

Their number has grown from the original fifteen to thirty-five and each year any member may sponsor a rookie who becomes a probationary member until he distinguishes himself with a bold and forthright act such as mooning the sheriff, entering the topless go-go contest at Mother Tucker's or jumping onto the

stage at the Red Carpet Lounge and stealing the entertainer's hat, as one desperate rookie had done the previous evening. "Oh, we got lawyers, accountants, factory workers, salesmen, bartenders, a heterogeneous mixing of fine fellows. We come from all over the country, Washington, Oregon, Davenport, Tallahassee."

I asked him about their uniform beer hats and sunglasses. "Oh, we all wear these so our families won't recognize us when they see us on TV."

I'd finished my beer, and I thanked the P.R. man for his time. "All part of the service," he said. "Here, have one of these." He handed me a cigar with a printed wrapper: The Qualls are the Balls. "We give one of these to each of the drivers. It's good for three miles an hour."

Their slogan is less facetious than perhaps even The Classics realize. Jerry Grant is running Indy for the ninth time, and it never gets any easier, he tells me. I remembered when we were racing together in the United States Road Racing Championship series in 1965, and Jerry had just run at Indy for the first time. "It's not really much different from road racing," he'd told me, "just more specialized, and all the turns go to the left." But he doesn't see it that way anymore. He's large for a racing driver, six three and over two hundred pounds. It's ninety-three degrees with matching humidity. The perspiration beads up on his forehead as he leans against the toolbench sipping a Fresca. "It's gotten so fast and so technically intricate here." His dark brown eyes fix on mine with a kind of intensity that seems at odds with the casual attitude of his body. They never seem to blink. "You remember when we were racing, how if the car wasn't handling quite right, you could drive it a different way, throw it into the corner a little differently and make up for the way the chassis was working. Well you can't do that here anymore. This race isn't really much different from any other race I run, but qualifying here is the greatest pressure I'm put under all year. Everything depends on those four laps, so much money and prestige and sponsorship. You just drive it the only way you can and hope everything's

Mario Andretti

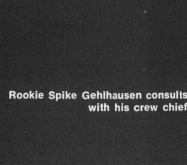
Rookie Spike Gehlhausen consults
with his crew chief

Frantic late-night last minute preparation in Gasoline Alley for first trials

Billy Vukovich and Gary Bettenhausen

Jerry Grant preparing to qualify

Billy Scott, the fastest rookie, 1976

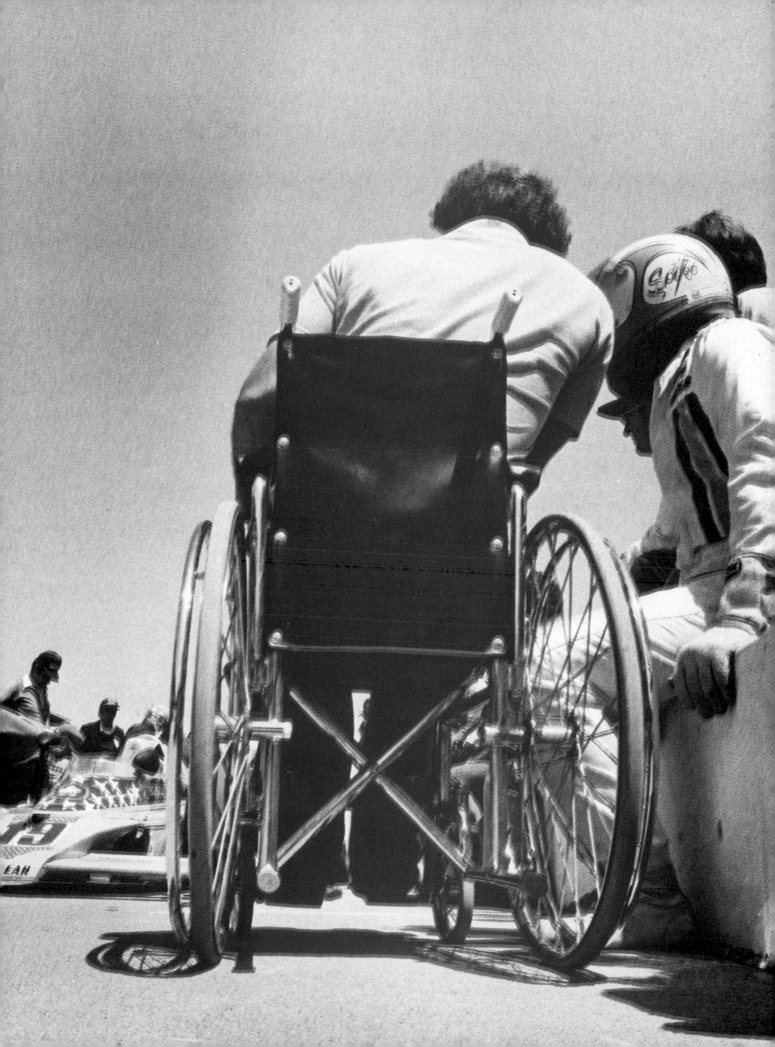

working for you, the car, the tires, the track, the air, cause if it isn't, there isn't much you can do about it."

In 1972, Grant qualified on the pole for the California 500 and was the first USAC driver to run an official qualification lap at over 200 mph, but today everything *isn't* working for him, and he qualifies fourteenth. Johnny Rutherford, who holds the one-lap record at Indianapolis and won the pole position in 1973, made the definitive statement on those four crucial laps after qualifying a disappointing 7 mph off the pace. "Some days you eat the bear, and some days the bear eats you."

It's a fairly reliable axiom that the best drivers will be offered the best cars, and rookies, unless they're already established superstars, consider themselves fortunate to have any kind of a ride for Indy. Usually they have to struggle with fairly antique and uncompetitive equipment. Billy Scott, the rookie for whom the driver's test at 170 mph had been, "a cakewalk," found that trying to push the same car just 12 mph a lap faster to make the race was a nightmare. And inferior equipment wasn't his only handicap. The intimidation of Indianapolis itself, the most important and tradition-bound race in the world, takes time and many laps of practice to overcome. "It's the biggest race in the world," Scott says. He leans close to be sure I can hear him over the din of the bar. "I saw those huge grandstands full of people watching me, and it suddenly hit me where I was. A couple of times it happened during practice. I'd start down the front straight and hear myself thinking, *Gee, I'm at Indy, I'm really at Indy.* Then I'd catch myself and say, *Cut that shit out and drive.* Finally I took an 869-foot spin coming out of turn three and ended up on the grass inside turn four. The car was okay, and so was I, but that really got my attention, like a dog shittin' a loggin' chain."

Scott failed to make competitive speed on two qualifying attempts and was waved off by his crew. The car owner decided to try another driver and put Graham McRae, an Indy veteran, in the car. But McRae's times were no better than Scott's. "I was pushing that car as fast as it was ever gonna go on this track," Scott explained, "but the old man wouldn't believe it." On his last attempt, Scott overcooked it coming out of turn four. The rear end came loose, and he made a spectacular spin down the front

26

straight, shedding fiber glass and suspension parts like a dog shaking water. "Too bad he didn't stuff it beyond fixin'," another driver quipped. "Now some other poor son of a bitch'll have to struggle with it next year."

I told Billy Scott about my friend Dave MacDonald who'd been killed eleven years earlier, coming out of turn four in an unstable car, how Jimmy Clark had followed him in practice and told him he should refuse to drive it in the race. "But I couldn't do that." Scott seemed shocked by the suggestion. "I mean if I stepped out of a ride, I'd never get another one. I'd be all washed up."

Billy Scott preparing for another practice run

Trhe thrill isn't there anymore." Andy Granatelli, who, with his legendary Novis and his turbine car that died four laps short of winning the 1967 race, has been responsible for more innovation and spectator interest than any other man in the Speedway's sixty-year history, looks tired and almost on the verge of tears as he talks about his twenty-nine-year lover's quarrel with Indianapolis. "Driving down here each year, I used to get so excited I'd start edging down on the accelerator, going faster and faster, till by the time I got to Lafayette I was driving flat out.

"But there's been too much tragedy," he explains, "that and USAC's continual legislation against innovation. It all comes down to the rules." He gets up and goes to the refrigerator for a can of diet pop. He's lost fifty pounds and waddles less conspicuously than he used to in those STP commercials. "Want one?" I accept. He pops the top, hands the can to me and sits back down at the end of the couch. "If they went to stock blocks, stock oil, stock gasoline and street available tires, you'd have a better race, and you'd have something about the cars the spectators could identify with."

"What about the changes they've made," I ask, "like wing restrictions and fuel limitations?"

"That's a start." He pauses for a swig of diet pop. "But they didn't go far enough. Look—he moves up on the edge of the couch and makes an expansive sweep with his hands—"you've got a governing board made up of twenty-one car owners, drivers and mechanics, all legislating their own interests. I mean, you ever see a committee of twenty-one that ever got anything done? No. What racing needs is a czar. Limit the fuel to two hundred gallons. You'd slow the cars down to one seventy, and you'd have a better race. The spectators wouldn't know the difference. They can't tell if a car's going two hundred or one fifty. You ever notice during qualifying, how they never cheer for the fastest cars till after they hear the time announced? They can't even see the drivers anymore, can't see their style or the way they drive, can't even see the numbers from the pits anymore.

"They killed my driver and my mechanic." There's a kind of forlorn intensity in his expression which, though he doesn't say it, pleads, *Don't you understand?* Two years earlier, the last year Granatelli entered the 500, Swede Savage, driving one of his cars,

was leading the race after 57 laps when he lost it coming out of
turn four, crashed brutally into the inside retaining wall and
suffered burns from which he was to die a month later. A Speedway
crash truck, rushing the wrong way up the pit lane, struck one of
Granatelli's crewmen from behind and killed him instantly. Those
in the pits, already horrified by the explosion and almost total
disintegration of Savage's car, saw the mechanic's body tossed
like a rag doll sixty feet in the air.

"Swede had just come out of the pits." Granatelli pauses
and draws his hand across his forehead. "He'd taken on eighty
gallons of fuel, and it was a completely different handling car than
he'd been driving a lap earlier."

To understand why Savage lost control in that particular
corner, it's necessary to speculate on what he must have been
thinking just before it happened.

Bobby Unser, who had previously been Savage's teammate,
had insulted him in print, had told the media that Savage couldn't
drive, that he wouldn't even include him on a list of the hundred
top drivers. Jerry Grant, who, like Unser, had been driving a white
Olsonite Eagle, explained it to me: "The track was oily, really
slippery in the groove, and Swedie was running high, making time
by staying above the groove where the track was dry. I think what
happened was that he saw a white car in his mirrors, and thought
Unser was closing on him. I guess he didn't realize it was me
and that Bobby was a lap down at that point. Anyway, he must
have been thinking about what Bobby had said about him, 'cause
he dove down into the groove to close the door on me. The car
was heavy with full fuel tanks, and he was just going too fast to
hold traction when he came down into the oil slick. It just must
have been brain fade. For a second there his mind must have been
somewhere else."

The race was stopped for an hour and fifteen minutes after
the crash, re-started and then called because of rain after 332
miles. Granatelli's other car, driven by Gordon Johncock, was
declared the winner, but it was a sad victory for Andy.

The diet pop can is empty now, and he sets it on the table
at the end of the couch. "Last year when we were coming in over
the airport, my wife looked down from the plane and saw the
Speedway. 'The thrill is gone, Andy,' that's what she said." He
looked down at the floor and tapped his chest. "It just isn't here
anymore."

Andy Granatelli (right) in Gasoline Alley

Dan Gurney is balancing on a small bicycle in the Jorgensen Steel garage in Gasoline Alley. I'm leaning against a workbench, and he seems to have me pinned in the corner with the flashing wheels of his unruly mount. He pulls up into an occasional wheely and I notice, with some relief, that the frame brace bar is thickly padded. "We can't forget we're in show business." His blue All-American Eagle rests unattended in the adjacent stall, race ready and immaculate. "We're competing for the entertainment dollar with football, baseball, hockey, whatever's going on at the same time, and those other things are more solidly entrenched and better organized than we are. I think that's the most important thing about this sport to keep in mind, even more important than the rules."

Like Andy Granatelli, Gurney feels the rules, as they now stand, are stifling championship car racing. "I'd like to see us get more in line with the rest of the world, go to the Grand Prix formula and get a full international sanction so we could attract foreign drivers again." I recalled Granatelli's complaint that Indy had become too homogeneous, that there were basically only two kinds of cars here anymore, the McLarens and Gurney's Eagles; and no more Jim Clarks, Graham Hills or Alberto Ascaris. "If we had foreign drivers here again," Gurney continues, "they'd have to build a third tier on the grandstands." He also wants to eliminate rules that favor turbochargers. "Turbocharged engines cut down the noise and the diversity of sounds and frankly, that's a big part of the spectator appeal."

I remind him that the Indianapolis 500 is already far and away the largest spectator event in the world.

"I know that," he smiles earnestly, "but that doesn't mean it couldn't be bigger." A man from ABC interrupts to tell Gurney they'd like to film an interview for *Wide World of Sports*. Dan politely explains that he's busy right now, and that he'll get to it as soon as he's free. I feel slightly impertinent, holding up ABC, like the flea with an erection who floats down the river, hollering for the drawbridge to be raised, but Gurney takes one thing at a time. While they are talking I notice three Indiana State troopers with nightsticks, Sam Browne belts and mirror-finish sunglasses in the bright alley beyond the garage door. I don't like to reinforce stereotypes, but they look polished, impersonal and just plain mean, like licensed bullies. Their presence is an integral part of the atmosphere of this race, as are the rioters, sadists, muggers, streakers, fornicators, motorcycle gangs, Frisbee players and drunks who occupy the infield like thirty armed tribes. The faint odor of tear gas is almost as common on race day as beer, popcorn and hot rubber. The man from ABC will wait outside with his crew.

"Where was I?" Dan smiles in apology for the interruption. "Okay, another thing about turbochargers is that they make the race so technologically intricate that it works against younger, less experienced drivers, so that you've got the same crop of forty-year-olds out there leading the race every year. We don't have a farm system like they do for Formula 1 racing, so there isn't a big crop of young fast drivers coming up all the time, pushing the older guys the way it is in Europe."

Dan's wife, Evi, walks into the garage and talks to Pete Biro, Gurney's P.R. man. The attention of the pit gawkers shifts from Dan and the car to a truly beautiful woman.

Bobby Unser signing autographs
for young fans

Dick Simon getting his car started
for his qualifying run

"What makes this race unique is tradition and the ripples that it causes all around the world. But what I don't like about it, and I guess it's a part of that tradition, is the amount of time we have to spend here. It's like a whole month in a police state." I smile and notice the troopers are talking with Bobby Unser, who the previous week had been made a special sheriff's deputy, had a police radio installed in his car and thirty minutes later, drove across town at unrecorded speeds to be the first on the scene to arrest three teenagers suspected of smoking marijuana behind an all-night market. "Maybe it's necessary for it to be that way in order to put this race on the way it is"—Gurney scratches his head and smiles wryly—"but we're all anxious to get back to the United States when it's over."

It's the morning of carburetion tests, three days before the race and the last opportunity any of the drivers will have to practice. I'm walking along Sixteenth Street toward the main gate to pick up my race-day credentials. I'm on a hard-packed dirt path just outside the chain-link fence that defines the official boundaries of the Speedway. Beyond the fence is a grass slope, a service vehicle road, then a rise, crested by the concrete retaining wall of the short chute between turns one and two. Above the wall is a catchfence woven of heavy steel cables, but the wall itself is low enough so that I can catch a glimpse of the wing, the windshield and the driver's helmet as he drifts to the wall setting up for turn two.

It's a hot morning. There aren't many spectators at the track today, and the traffic on Sixteenth Street is relatively light. There's a deceptively relaxed atmosphere as this day begins. Qualifying is over, and the tension seems to have subsided. I hear the Doppler effect of an engine, wound tight and rising down the front straight. It's getting louder, then seems to fade momentarily behind the grandstands on turn one. Suddenly it rises again, then, *Zap*, one startling reverberation off the wall, one strobelike flash of sunlight off orange and white, and it's past, powering into turn two, the pitch rising and fading down the back straight. My stomach tightens. The sheer speed has given me a light punch in the solar plexus and a prickly sensation all over my skin, and I realize how much of that sense of speed is lost on television; telephoto lenses and elevated camera angles convey the impression of a relaxed, almost slow-motion kind of game.

Television has come a long way in transcribing sports action on a field, court or track to a circumscribed image composed of dots and spaces on a screen, capable of a multitude of points of view, *but* again, only one at a time. After several years of experimentation, they've learned to photograph tennis matches so that you can actually see both the players and the ball. The same can be said of football. With slow-motion instant replays you can have a more detailed, though still particularized, look at every bone-jarring nuance in your living room, bedroom or bar, than

any ticket-buying, pennant-waving, crowd-braving fan in the stadium. But they haven't quite pulled it off with motor racing. They've got it down to covering every turn, accident and pit stop, interviewing drivers and crews and explaining the particular challenges and characteristics of each track. But the one thing they haven't yet been able to adequately capture is speed.

Anyone who has gotten out and gone to a race after watching them on television is astounded at how fast the cars zoom past him. Maybe part of it's being there with the ear-splitting engine noise, the smell of rubber, oil and asphalt, but when you get out from behind the telephoto lens and see how long those straights really are and how little time it takes a racing car to cover the seemingly immense distance from turn four to turn one, it causes a certain physical sensation in the scalp and at the base of the spine that television viewers never know. "My God, they're going fast." It's no longer the sort of leisurely motorized game you've watched between commercials. You feel the ground shudder under your feet, and it feels a little threatening.

But maybe the camera is better than the naked eye at projecting the driver's experience of speed. Of course there are vibrations, sounds and G-force sensations that the driver alone can experience, but when a man lives long enough at 200 mph, 200 mph become the norm, and he slows it down. Through his eyes, as long as he remains in control, things don't happen with the frightening rapidity with which we would perceive them. For him, the track isn't a chaotic blur, but a calmly perceived series of sensations now, now, now and now. He fixes on nothing and is therefore not startled by the brevity of his relationship with any object in the field of his experience. It's a kind of Zen by default in which survival depends upon nonattachment and single-mindedness, a gestalt from which no element can be removed and examined.

L. B. CLARKE I.M.C.
TWO RIVERS PUBLIC SCHOOLS

Johnny Rutherford beginning a practice pit stop

Most of the drivers would like to get on with it. The field is set, but tradition dictates the week-long waiting game between the end of qualifying and race day. Today's carburetion tests are the only chance they'll have to get back on the track until they line up for the parade lap preceding the race. Today they are given three hours to get in a little more practice, make a last-minute check of carburetion and tires, experience how the car will handle on race day with a full fuel load, and one hour to practice pit stops.

Twenty years ago a forty-five-second pit stop to refuel and change tires would have been considered highly efficient, but today it would be a disaster, costing the driver almost a lap and probably putting him out of contention. The Gatorade McLaren team pulls Johnny Rutherford's car back up the pit lane, then pushes it in to simulate a pit stop. Each member of the crew is waiting in his assigned position, tires, jacks, impact wrenches, refueling hoses ready. For Rutherford it means practice in stopping exactly on his marks. During the race he'll be coming down the pit lane at almost 100 mph and must sight his crew and bring the car to a stop precisely at the spot where each crew member can do his job without having to change position. Tyler Alexander, the crew chief, stands in the pit lane to mark the point where the nose of the car should come to rest. Rutherford stops exactly on the mark, and five men go to work. The refueling and vent nozzles are inserted, impact wrenches twist off the right-hand hub nuts, a jack instantly lifts the right side of the car, two wheels are removed and replaced with another set, the jack is removed and the tires come back to the pavement. The impact wrenches blast again, the refueling nozzles are removed, the front-tire man

Jerry Grant's crew practices pit stop

jumps out of the way, whipping his airhose clear of the car. I duck to avoid a mechanic as he hurtles over the wall. Only five men are allowed in the pit during a stop and a sixth man has offered Rutherford a cup of water at the end of a rod extended from behind the pit wall. Rutherford has never taken his eyes off Alexander. Three crew members fall in behind the car, Alexander waves him off and the car is pushed back into the pit lane. Teddy Mayer clicks his digital stopwatch: 12.5 seconds from the instant the car stopped until the wheels are rolling again.

Normally, most of the pit stops would be for fuel only. The crew would check the right-side tires and be prepared to change them if necessary. In Jerry Grant's pit, they've made five practice stops with tire changes and simulated refueling, the same procedure again and again until it's become a mechanical routine. A sixth time Grant coasts to a stop, but now he pulls a surprise and points to the left front tire, a frantic series of stabs with his index finger. The front man scurries around to the other side of the car and undoes the nut while the jack man moves to jack up the left side. When the tire man has changed the tire and secured the nut, he scrambles back to the right side of the car and gives Grant the all-clear signal. When the practice stop is completed, Grant motions the front-tire man over to confer with him. They've handled the unexpected tire change flawlessly and without hesitation, but Grant figures it has taken the tire changer an extra second or two to get back to the right front corner of the car to give his all-clear signal. The tire man kneels by the cockpit while Grant tells him to give the signal from the left side of the car in case they have to change the left-front tire.

Adrenaline will be running freely when the actual pit stops are made and the tension can be felt in this last bit of practice before race day. The driver will be sitting with the car in gear, the engine running and the clutch in, and it's crucial that he has only one crewman to look to for his signals, that there are no misunderstandings. I remembered seeing films of Parnelli Jones rolling on the pavement in invisible alcohol flames after a botched pit stop. Thinking he'd been given the all clear, he'd pulled away from his pit with the fuel hose still connected, rupturing the tank, eliminating himself from the race, sustaining some painful burns and causing a potentially dangerous situation in the entire pit and front straight grandstand area.

I looked up and down the row of refueling tanks mounted on scaffolds above the pit wall and realized that on race day I'd rather be anywhere else on the track. One 240-gallon tank of highly combustible methanol fuel for each of the thirty-three cars, and it would take only one careless act, one car out of control in the pit lane to cause a chain reaction that could endanger hundreds of lives. "I'm surprised something like that's never happened," one driver confided. "I feel a whole lot safer out on the track than I do during a pit stop. It's not just the time lost from

Rick Muther and his non-qualifying Joe Hunt special

Rick Muther

A non-qualifying car is converted into a bar in Jim Hurtubise's garage

the race; I'm really anxious to get away from all that fuel and confusion."

Tradition dominates every aspect of Indianapolis, and not only in a ceremonial sense. There is a pervading attitude among those in authority that there is a *right way* of doing things and that way has acquired its mantle of rectitude by virtue of the fact that "It *is* the way we do it." Actually it may be the only way they are able to run this race, dealing with a group of men as egocentric and opinionated as racing drivers. "I don't know" is a statement seldom heard. Whichever aspect of race procedure is in question, each of them will not only have an answer, he will have *the* answer, and a dictator behind the badge of a Chief Steward is required.

Refueling tanks and the penalty for jacking to get the last bit of fuel from them is the first order of business at the driver's and crew chief's meeting following pit practice. It's a Turkish bath. The main concourse below the tower is packed with rows of folding chairs and sealed off to the public as well as to ventilation by Speedway guards. Spectators press their faces against the glass doors, blocking the reflections of the afternoon sunlight with their cupped hands. From inside the meeting room, they look like visitors to an aquarium. Tom Binford, the Chief Steward, calls the meeting to order. His situation is similar to that of the President of the United States at a news conference, both man on the spot and the ultimate authority.

With each car limited to 280 gallons for the race, fuel and its handling become a controversial issue. Even if a car could mechanically withstand being driven flat out for the entire five hundred miles, with a consumption rate of between 1.2 and 1.4 miles per gallon, it would eliminate itself by running out of fuel in the process. Most of the teams, particularly those of the front runners, will be depending on a certain amount of the race being run under yellow light conditions in order to be able to stretch their allotted fuel over the distance. Binford settles the refueling controversy as soon as the meeting has been called to order. Refueling tanks may be mounted at an incline of eleven degrees. Pit stewards will check the angle of incline and any tanks exceeding this angle, or any tanks jacked during the race will be cause for disqualification. This will be the most definite ruling made during the entire meeting. Almost all other aspects of race procedure seem to be open to a certain variance of interpretation, and Binford generally chooses to let the penalties for infractions remain vague.

An argument over the use of pacer lights for regulating speed in a yellow light situation occupies almost half the meeting time. A. J. Foyt, Bobby Unser, and Mario Andretti argue that while the pacer lights were a good idea, they just don't seem to work. They would prefer the use of the pace car to control speed in an emergency situation even though it would allow the field to close its distance on the leaders.

"The pacer lights stay," Binford states flatly.

"Well hell"—Foyt is on his feet—"those lights screwed up the other day during practice. They got sequenced over two hundred miles an hour, and I had to scurry the hell outta myself try'n to keep up with 'em." Everyone but Binford laughs.

Grant King, a car builder and crew chief, argues that since most of the drivers would prefer the pace car, why not reinstate it and forget the light system.

Binford, "Because the regulations call for the pacer lights."

King, "But none of these rules are irrevocable."

Binford, "I know that, but the Speedway management prefers the lights." End of controversy.

Bobby Unser is up again, contending that since name drivers like "me and Al and A. J. and Mario are better known and get watched closer than these other guys, we get unfairly penalized for yellow light infractions."

"I guess that's the price of fame." Binford seems unmoved.

Someone raises the question about onboard fuel capacity, covertly referring to the controversy stemming from George Bignotti's insinuations that Foyt had carried an extra five-gallon fuel tank somewhere in his car during the California 500. Binford appears to have been expecting this one and states that they have already made plans to inspect the fuel capacity of the first ten finishers.

Grant King wants to know what the penalty will be for having too many men over the wall during a pit stop. Binford takes a deep breath and wipes his forehead. "Any crew with more than five men over the wall will be penalized accordingly."

"Well I want to know exactly what that penalty's going to be," King insists, "because if it's only gonna be a fifty-dollar fine, I'm going to have fifteen men over that wall."

Binford assures him that it will be more than a fifty-dollar fine. He wipes his forehead again.

It seems the room is getting hotter, and I half expect a huge hand to reach in through the doorway and poke me with a fork to see if I'm done. Jerry Grant sips his Fresca. James Garner whispers to Al Unser and Mario Andretti, and all three smile knowingly.

Foyt stands up again, his arms bulging from his short-sleeved sport shirt. He looks impatient and impressive. He always looks impatient and impressive, on or off the track. Several nights earlier, I watched him make his entrance in the Speedway Motel dining room. He seated his wife and walked over to another table to talk with four men, aware that every eye was on him. It had been almost as if a tiger had wandered into the room, and while nobody wanted to make a scene about it, nobody wanted to lose track of where he was. Foyt asks Binford whether or not Goodyear technicians will be allowed over the wall to check tires during pit stops.

Binford, "No, not if they make the total more than five."

"Well hell, you talk about safety, those Goodyear people are a hell of a lot better judges of whether a tire needs changing than any of these mechanics."

Binford concedes the point. Tire technicians will be

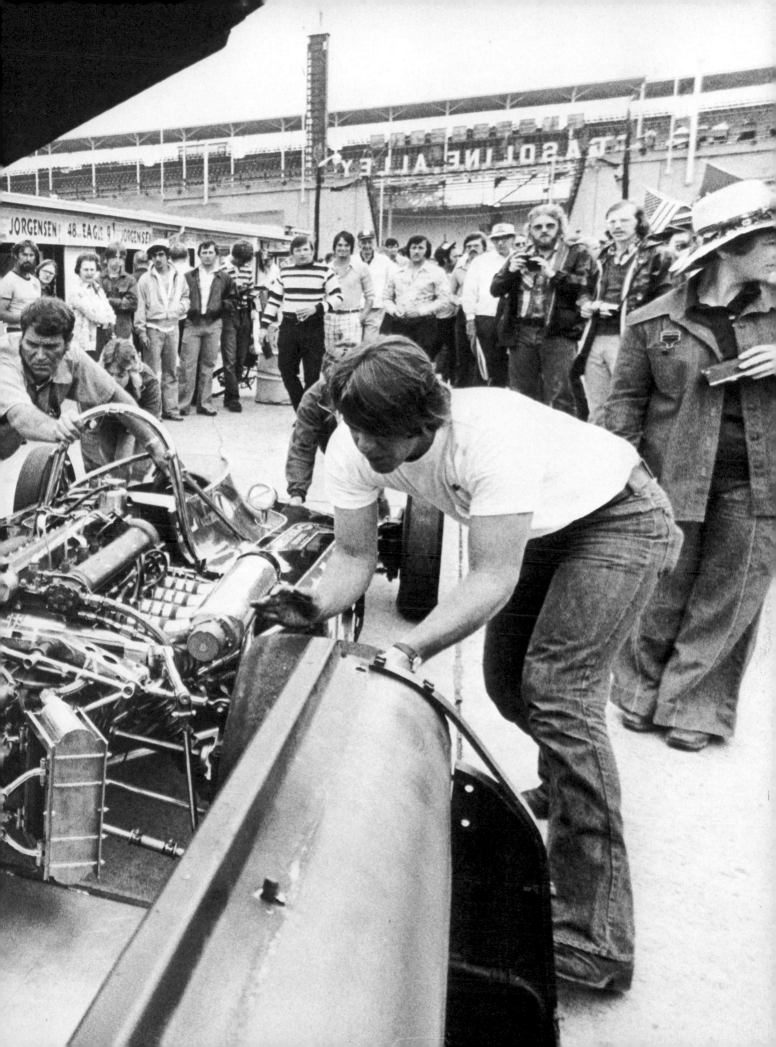

allowed. But that doesn't sit well with Billy Vukovich. "But what if I don't have any Goodyear men in my pit, then it isn't fair."

"You start runnin' out there in front"—Foyt twists the knife—"and you'll have so many of 'em you'll be wantin to trade 'em off." A wave of laughter spreads through the meeting and then dies away uncomfortably. Salt Walther asks what the penalty will be for improving your position prior to crossing the starting line. I can see the black glove on his left hand, the full use of which he lost in a crash at the start of the 1973 race, a crash initiated by a charging car that bumped him into the outside retaining wall. It's an important question, and a pointed one coming from Walther. Binford states that anyone flagrantly charging before the starting line will be penalized one lap. He goes on to urge everyone not to really start racing until they've come out of turn two and started down the back straight.

"Look," he pleads, "for most of us, our livelihoods and our careers are centered around this one race, and it'd be stupid and pointless to spoil it by getting overanxious at the start of it."

The meeting adjourns with Binford asking several of the name drivers to stay for a briefing of the rookies. At speeds well over 200 mph, the "old boy–new boy" system is a vital part of the Indy tradition. There's a big show coming up in three days, the biggest one in sports, and it has to be made absolutely clear to the rookies how they are expected to play their parts.

Janet Guthrie

48

Failing to qualify for the 1976 race, Janet heads back to her garage

It's the evening before the race, and Speedway, Indiana, has become a refugee camp. Every field and vacant lot within miles is packed with trailers, tents, motor homes, sweating bodies, piles of empty beer cans, and backyard barbecues. Refugee camps are better organized. These are the Mongol hordes, the Huns awaiting race day to storm the gates of Rome. Campfires glow. I'm certain I can hear the throbbing of tribal drums, unintelligible chanting. Police sirens are as commonplace as the random explosions of cherry bombs. A prison bus with heavily wire-meshed windows speeds past in a clusteral escort of flashing lights. There will be a total eclipse of the moon tonight and it seems to hype the lunacy. Except for a few nervous mechanics and staff personnel, the Speedway is empty and quiet. From a helicopter it would look like a black oval, a void in a galaxy of fire and chaos.

The motel room I'm sharing with Bob Jones faces Sixteenth Street and is less than one hundred feet from an entrance to the track. It's a convenient bivouac, but only a self-hypnotist could sleep here. During the evening several gaggles of girls from tent city have wandered in to use our bathroom. Invariably their introductory line is "Knock, knock" —the door is open—"I know it's a terrible imposition, but this is an emergency."

This one sits down and has a cigarette while her companion uses the plumbing. I offer her a drink, and Jones interrogates her. She's from Indianapolis and claims she's twenty-one, though sixteen seems more likely. When she laughs, she snorts through her sinuses and she laughs at almost everything she says. "You guys got any spare change?" She laughs at this too.

"No, none that's spare."

"You're selfish."

Jones asks her if she left a dime in the bathroom. "Oh that," she says. "But I left something else." She finds this funny too. Jones and I are infected by her laughter and laugh at ourselves because there's nothing to laugh at.

"What do you think about the race?" It's a rhetorical question.

"What race?" She snorts again and we all laugh.

I nod over my shoulder in the direction of the Speedway. She covers her lips with her cupped hand and snorts a mouthful of vodka and tonic through her fingers. "I don't even know who's racing."

I ask her why she's here, and she says it's for the crowd in the camp across the street. "It's the most exciting thing that happens all year. Ya live in Indianapolis, this is like Christmas, it's what ya wait for." I was reminded of all the middle-aged, middle-class women I'd seen cruising the bar at the Holiday Inn, doctors', lawyers' and salesmen's wives, race groupies for whom the race means only a chance to meet a stranger, a mechanic, a tire buster or a P.R. man, maybe from far-off, exotic California. There were also 150,000 fans who would fill the infield, most of whom, by mid-afternoon, would have forgotten why they'd come there in the first place.

Now the other girl has finished in the bathroom. "Ya know we don't have to go," the snort queen offers. "I mean we could stay here."

"You could, but you can't." I hear the crackle of radios from the police cruisers along the street and encourage them to go back to tent city.

Although the gates won't open until 5:00 A.M., the traffic starts stacking up shortly after midnight. I close the door, turn out the lights and lie awake with the sirens, honking horns, motorcycle engines and the anticipation of the race. I wonder how well the drivers are sleeping, or if they are.

I realize I must have finally fallen asleep, because I'm awakened at 6:30 by an immense pounding on the door. I swing my feet to the floor and sit for a minute trying to remember where I am and to determine whether or not I'd been dreaming. I open the door on the long shadows of early morning light. The traffic is still solid and the police radios still crackle unintelligible messages. I've almost forgotten why I opened the door when someone grabs my right hand. "Hi, I'm Dayton Spengler. It's a beautiful day, and it's time for you boys to get up and go to work." A puffy, almost featureless, florid face, little pig eyes squinting out from under the visor of a white yachting cap. "You boys do a good job now."

"Thank you." I turn and close the door. Jones is still snoring. *Maybe it's a special wake-up service the motel has for race day,* I thought. I'd promised Heinz Kluetmeier that I'd cover turn two with one of his motor-drive Nikons, so it did make sense. I did have a job to do. I looked at the camera on top of the dresser and had a momentary apprehension that I'd already missed something important. I had barely settled back onto the sheets again when the pounding resumed.

"Hi!" My hand was being pumped again. "You remember me. I'm Dayton Spengler."

"Sure." It was true, I did remember him.

"Say, this lady's kinda sick and I wonder if she could use your room to lie down a little while." I peered around the doorjamb in the direction he indicated, and the blonde lady with the beehive hairdo seemed bored and impatient. She was pretending to be interested in the traffic on Sixteenth Street and refused to acknowledge either Dayton or me.

"Well gee." I stumbled for a moment trying to figure out what I'd do while she was using my room and how I'd explain it to Jones. After all, Jones didn't even know him. Then Jones himself helped me out.

"No." I looked over my shoulder and saw the whites of his eyes glowing through the dark cave of the room. They didn't look the least bit sympathetic toward my friend Dayton's cause.

"No," I said.

"Well, that's okay." My hand was being pumped again. "You boys have a good day."

I closed the door and looked at Jones. He was laughing. "That's Indy," he said. "There's your story."

At nine o'clock, two hours before race time, I head over to the track. I'd been given a pass to shoot photographs from the balcony of the Penske Suite overlooking turn two. It's a precarious, though very pleasant, setup. Drinks, snacks and air conditioning will be available a few steps away and the view of the short chute, turn two and the back straight is excellent, though I'll be sitting less than twenty feet from the edge of the track at the point where the cars begin to exit the turn. I'd felt a little exposed there watching qualifying, feeling the vibration and heat from the passing cars and gauging the strength of the cables reinforcing the wire fence that was all that separated me from the track. I had reminded myself that it was only steel cables that held up the Golden Gate Bridge, and that if they did fail, anything that happened would happen so fast that I wouldn't have time to torment myself with the hope of escape.

On the telephone that morning my nine-year-old son asked me to get the autograph of the winner. "It's not likely I'll be able to get close to him after the race," I told him. "Why don't you just pick a driver whose autograph you'd like and I'll get that." There was a long silence at the other end of the line while he searched for a name, then a tentative "Is Bobby Unser there?" I pull a small photograph of Unser from the *Jorgensen Eagle* press kit, slip it between the pages of a program to keep it from getting bent and set off for the pits with a pre-race mission.

A few steps from the door of my room I can feel the juices begin to ooze from my skin and I expect to deliquesce like a maple-sugar doll. In the pedestrian tunnel that crosses under the track I fall in with a half-dozen slightly flaccid, halter-topped high school girls. They have already begun to pink a bit on the back and shoulders and somehow smell like school lunch boxes, the redolence of overripe bananas. I am now part of the great event, a drone filing into the hive, *the people, yes,* and so goddam many of them, hippies, rednecks, straights and hoods. We are passed by a seemingly endless line of Buick convertibles carrying celebrities and race queens. I don't recognize any of the celebrities, though we scatter before them like peasants before the coaches of the king. At least a dozen bands are playing, and the atmosphere is already so bizarre that I half expect to see a guillotine in the next parting of the crowd. I'm concentrating on my own pace, trying to maintain some identity, trying not to fall in step with the martial music of whichever band is dominating the moment. But the crowd is moving in time, and I must move with it or be trampled. The Golden Girl of the Purdue Band is attracting all the photographers, who a moment before had been three deep around A. J. Foyt as he checked over his safety harness and every detail in the cockpit of his Gilmore Coyote. Most of the drivers are staying in their garages, avoiding the crowds and the heat as long as they can. The pit lane looks like Fifth Avenue on Easter Sunday, two ill-defined columns of aimless strollers with pit badges in lieu of bonnets, there to see and to be seen.

The pit crowd is noticeably better groomed than those in the infield, crews in bright-colored uniforms, photographers in bush jackets under tiers of Nikons and car owners, sponsors and officials in seersucker suits. I feel a little underdressed in my Levi's and short-sleeved cotton shirt. I decide it's time to head

Gasoline Alley after the rain

across the infield toward the suites. I cut through Gasoline Alley and stop by Gurney's garage to get Bobby Unser's autograph. There doesn't seem to be a great deal of tension in the garage. It's an hour until race time and Unser is still dressed in blue cotton trousers and a short-sleeved shirt. He gladly signs my photograph and seems relaxed, as if there was nothing special he had to do. Then it occurs to me that there isn't anything special he has to do. If you are a professional racing driver, driving races is what you do, and he's done it almost every week for the last twenty-six years. Indianapolis may be the biggest race around, but still a race is a race. I thank him for the autograph and remember not to wish him good luck. There are so many uncontrollable variables in racing that drivers tend to be superstitious, and being wished good luck is one curse they'd rather do without. I pass Jerry Grant's garage and think of stopping to wish him good luck without saying it, but the doors are closed and I figure he'd rather be alone. I remember that when I was driving I'd never really had anything to say to anyone before a race. Any conversation that occurred was like that at a Christian Science funeral, about anything but the business at hand.

A few Frisbees are being tossed on the infield golf course, a few couples are making love in the sand traps and the sweet aroma of marijuana hangs in the breezeless air.

At the Penske suite, the chairman of the bank whose travelers' checks have cosponsored the Penske McLaren driven by Tom Sneva, extends himself to make me feel welcome, points out the bar and buffet, tells me not to hesitate to ask for whatever I need. He even suggests that I might be able to bribe the maintenance man to show me how to get up on the roof. "Anything we can do for you, anything at all, just sing out and it'll be done." A hearty clap on the shoulder. His graciousness seems quite genuine, though I am beginning to realize that my motor-driven Nikon and *Sports Illustrated* nametag represent some fairly heavy credentials. I stake out a seat on the corner of the balcony where no one would be moving between my lens and the track, fix myself a tonic water and check my focus and exposure. There are no rednecks or hippies here in the suites, a madras and La Costa crowd, collegians of the fifties with a few crow's-feet and gray hairs, not surprisingly, the kind of people one would associate with Roger Penske, precise and successful.

The prerace ceremonies have begun, the celebrities have been driven around the track, Peter DePaolo, winner of the 1925 500, has taken a lap in the Miller that won the race in 1930, the Speedway has been presented with a plaque designating it as a national historic landmark and the final lines of the invocation drift across the infield, "...with a hand over the heart, a prayer in the soul and brains in the head." Now everything seems to accelerate, including four hundred thousand pulse rates. Jim Nabors mouths every word of "Back Home Again in Indiana," a thousand helium-filled balloons are released, Tony Hulman takes the microphone. "Gentlemen, start your *in*juns." The parade and pace laps come off without incident. Some of the drivers wave or salute as they pass the suites of their sponsors. I am reminded of knights dipping their lances to the ladies whose favors they wore. The ritual hasn't changed, only become more commercial. I know

Mario Andretti with the latest development in tricycles

the drivers are very calm now. For them the prerace tension is over and they are locked into that impenetrable concentration that comes the moment they are strapped into the car. As they approach the starting line, everyone becomes very quiet, probably the one moment when not one of the nearly half-million people in this arena has anything to say. The engine noise accelerates, a series of bombs explode in the air, and a great cheer goes up from the crowd. The announcer's voice booms, "And the fifty-ninth Indianapolis 500-Mile Race is under way, the greatest spectacle in racing."

After the start and the excitement of the initial laps, the race, for most of the spectators, diminishes to a monotonous stream of almost indistinguishable cars and anonymous drivers flowing by at over 200 mph. I don't mean that it isn't still exciting. The noise itself is enough to keep the adrenaline pumped up, but you have to rely on the track announcer to understand what's happening. It's very much the way it was all those years I listened to it on the radio, but with a lot of special effects thrown in. I'm aware that Johncock, who had jumped into a commanding lead at the start, has dropped out. It's a 500-mile race. Running away with the early laps may please the crowd and momentarily put a driver in the limelight, but the chances are he'll be all but forgotten when the checkered flag falls. Foyt and Rutherford are swapping the lead now, though I'm seldom certain who has it at any given moment. As the cars scream out of turn two it all seems effortless, though they're fighting the limit of adhesion. They pass so close it almost seems I could touch them. In twos and threes, the engines surge down the back straight like aircraft engines out of sync.

There's a yellow light and most of the cars head for the pits. For a full ten seconds no cars pass, and the silence is startling. I'm keeping my camera ready, watching what's coming out of turn two and trying to answer the questions of the distractingly pretty lady who has taken the seat next to me. Our conversation is disjointed, broken sentences sequenced in the brief intervals between passing cars. Occasionally a whiff of her perfume mingles with and subsumes the perspiration and burning rubber. She's a young Grace Kelly type from somewhere in Pennsylvania. It's difficult to hear, let alone remember, details in these circumstances. She seems unaffected by the heat, which at the moment is causing large drops of sweat to trickle over my ribs. They tickle, and I know if I touch them they'll show through my shirt. I want to appear to be as cool as she is. I lean closer for her next question, but not too close. At the same time I'm reminding myself to keep my lens and my attention on turn two.

Several times I stand up to watch some passing action down the back straight. Tom Sneva is running a highly respectable fifth and is still very much in contention. He pulls to the inside to lap several slower cars and the precision of his judgment keeps me standing. It seems he won't have time to get past them and back into the groove to set up for turn three, and I realize that at that point he's traveling at about 220 mph. He's deep, almost too deep, but in the last few feet, he cuts back to the outside, clear of the traffic and right in the groove. Then I remembered how it always looked more impressive from the outside than it does from

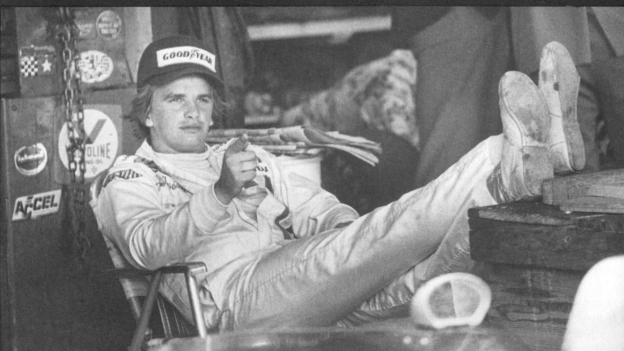

Spike Gehlhausen in his garage looking confident

the driver's seat. Once at Mosport, during practice for the Canadian Grand Prix, I walked over to watch at turn one while my car was being worked on. I was frightened and astounded at how ragged and perilous it seemed, the cars skidding and vibrating through the reverse camber downhill turn. *Jesus, that's scary*, I thought. *How can they do it*? then a half hour later went and qualified on the pole for the G. T. race. I didn't know *how* to do it. I just did it.

More laps, more questions, more fragmented answers: "They're limited to"—two cars scream through the turn, nose to tail and I wait for the noise to fade—"280 gallons which means that"—another car passes and I can feel the heat from its exhaust—"at the mileage they're getting that they"—this time we're interrupted by the track announcer calling attention to Wally Dallenbach who started in twenty-first position and is now moving up toward the lead at an alarming rate—"they couldn't finish the race if they didn't do at least"—another car—"a few laps under the yellow."

I've been watching Dallenbach. His engine sounds stronger, higher pitched and wound tighter than the other cars, and another strange thing is that though he's gobbling up the field, his line through the corners isn't following the groove. He's running through the middle of turn two each time he passes, not drifting wide and using the whole track the way other cars do when they're turning hot laps. Each time he passes, it seems he's operating on a separate principle of physics, as if the laws governing centrifugal force had been suspended for him. Later I would hear rumblings that he had a small tank of nitrous oxide (laughing gas) that was being injected directly into the cylinders, giving him an extra 150 horsepower with no increase in boost, and that his unorthodox line was to compensate for the extra sensitivity under his right foot. It occurred to me that if that were true, it might be possible that the nitrous oxide was being injected directly into Dallenbach and that his extra speed was the result of an altered consciousness. Whatever the facts, Dallenbach was laughing on the 60th lap when he passed Foyt and went on to open up a 22-second lead.

One hundred and twenty-six laps and almost two hours of racing. Senses are beginning to numb and the stream of cars is beginning to have a hypnotic effect on the afternoon. I have a mild headache, my throat's getting sore and fortunately, or unfortunately, Grace Kelly is asking fewer questions. The tension begins to dissolve into monotony. I'm less attentive with my lens and have pretty well determined that I won't have to shoot any action on this turn today. Somebody taps me on the shoulder and as I turn to my right I hear a scream from the crowd, followed by a loud dull thud. I turn back to my left and there, not forty feet away and twenty feet in the air, just above eye level, is the top of Tom Sneva's helmet. Flames have engulfed the rear half of his car and it's cartwheeling horizontally along the wire-retaining fence. I have

a stop-action image, looking at the car as if from above as it hurtles toward me, but not on film. I've forgotten about my camera. For an instant I am certain I'm witnessing a man's death and that it will also be my own. Things have gone too smoothly, the atmosphere has been deceptively benign, and it now seems this track has demanded another catastrophe. I leap over the now vacant chair to my right, and as I turn toward the suite, I see the reflection of the flames in the sliding glass doors and feel the heat sweep across my back. The instant of danger has passed and I turn back toward the track just in time to see the disembodied engine tumble by in a ball of flame. Debris fills the air like a flight of sand grouse. The Nikon takes over, zipping off exposures like a digital computer, one last somersault before the car comes to rest, right side up and on fire. It really doesn't resemble a car anymore, just a burning tub of metal, not thirty feet away, a driver's helmet protruding from the flames. The original fire had been from burning oil, but now the methanol has ignited and can be seen only as intense heat waves blurring the edges of the wreckage.

The fire marshall is herding everyone off the balconies and into the suites. He sees my camera and press badge and lets me stay, though I've finished the roll and have to change film. At this point, I'm certain Sneva is dead. It's the most brutal, spectacular and horrifying crash I've ever seen, and I've seen at least a dozen that were fatal. The scene in the suite couldn't be more macabre or more comic. All these people know Sneva in some capacity. Several of them are the sponsors of his car, and he's crashed and apparently been annihilated right in their laps. Sneva's wife has gone into hysterics and has been hustled out to the balcony overlooking the golf course on the far side of the building. Grace Kelly, who had been fixing a drink at the time, had fallen backward and sat in a tray of chocolate brownies. The chairman of the bank, in nervous relief, tells me how delighted he is that I've been able to get good pictures. Though I'm sure it isn't his intention, it sounds as if, in his role as gracious host, he has arranged the crash for my photographic convenience. Everyone looks sick to their stomachs, and I am changing film.

"Did you get it?" I look up into the wide eyes of a young executive type.

"Ya, I think so."

"Did you get Mrs. Sneva?"

"What?" I'm certain I've misunderstood.

"Did you get pictures of Mrs. Sneva?"

I choke on my own saliva and shake my head. "I didn't hear that. No."

"Good for you," he says earnestly, "good for you."

The fire marshall lets me back out on the balcony to photograph the work of the fire crew. There are clouds of chemical vapors, flashing lights, scattered detritus and crash crews diverting traffic to the grass verge inside the track. Then I see something that, for a moment, I am certain is an illusion. Sneva moves. His helmet is wiggling back and forth and he's put his arms down on the fuselage, trying to push himself up and out of the cockpit, but he appears to be stuck. Another driver has abandoned his car and is trying to help the emergency crew get Sneva out of the wreckage. The struggle goes on for several

minutes till they finally free him, dragging him up and out by his armpits. Not only is he alive, but he walks, with help, to the waiting ambulance, lies down on the stretcher and is taken to the infield hospital. Still I'm not confident he'll recover. I remember how two years before Swede Savage had ridden to the infield hospital sitting up, but died of his injuries a month later.

The emergency crew finishes clearing the debris, and I sit down to try and sort out what has happened. It is at that moment that I realize that two weeks earlier, to the hour, I had been sitting on this balcony interviewing Tom Sneva the day after he had qualified. He told me he had been a junior high school principal in Lamont, Washington, and had raced as a hobby until the racing began to be more profitable and more time-consuming than teaching. He was enthusiastic, boyish and articulate and appeared to regard Roger Penske with almost the same reverence that a University of Alabama quarterback might hold for Bear Bryant. "We'd like to be racing more than just the Championship Trail," he tells me, "but Roger's got a lot invested in this series, and he doesn't want to take any chances." He reminded me how the previous year Penske lost his driver in mid-season when Gary Bettenhausen was seriously injured in a minor dirt-track race in Syracuse. I asked him about his relationship with the established superstars like Foyt and Unser. "That's a funny thing," he said. There was surprise in his voice, as if he were only discovering the irony as he told me about it. "I guess they just thought of us as another kid who wanted to be a racing driver. Anyway, they barely paid any attention to us, hardly said hello, until we began to become a threat to them." I asked him why he referred to himself in the plural, and he said it was a habit. "It's a team effort. If we win I don't want to take all the credit, and if we lose, I don't want all the blame." I'm sure this *organization man* attitude is largely the result of driving for a no-nonsense, quasi-military business organization like Penske's, but there also seems to be a certain element of the affectionate plurality with which a show jumper will refer to himself and his horse as one being. "Anyway," Sneva continued, "when we started showing them something, that indifference seemed to change; not that they got friendly or anything, but they knew we were there."

I had first become aware of Sneva while watching a television broadcast of the Phoenix 150 several years ago. I remembered having been quite impressed watching this then unknown driver pass Foyt to take the lead. As we sat there that overcast afternoon, he told me the story. "Foyt was having a little momentary problem with his car. He bobbled, and I shot by him like he was standing still. It was no big deal. He was having trouble for a second, and I took advantage of it and got by. But they played it up big on television, as if I'd really pulled something off. Anyway, Foyt wasn't upset about it after the race but later, when people, friends of his who'd watched it on TV, razzed him about it, 'Boy, that Sneva kid really blew you off, didn't he?' he began to get pissed. Then one day he walked up to me in the garage—I mean it was just like something out of the movies—and told me that I'd gotten away with it this once, but that if I tried anything like it again, he could bump me right out of the park. It was unbelievable."

The ABC slow-motion replays showed Sneva passing Eldon Rasmussen and running just ahead of Foyt in the short chute between turns one and two. Sneva's right rear tire touched Rasmussen's left front, and Sneva found himself upside down and airborne, heading for the outside wall at almost two hundred miles an hour. Sneva's car slams into the wall tail first, the wing, engine and rear wheels separating, in a protracted dance with the flames and scattering fragments of metal and fiber glass; the remains of the car cartwheeling three times along the wall, then somersaulting three times down the asphalt to come to rest, on fire, in the middle of the track. It's the kind of accident usually associated with dirt tracks at less than half these speeds.

Three weeks later, Sneva is recovering from his burns and practicing to qualify for the 500 at Pocono when I talk to him on the telephone. "It was like a dream," he tells me. "We watched the TV replays and it looked like it was all happening to somebody else. We passed Rasmussen in the first turn and thought we were by him in turn two. We glanced in the mirrors and he wasn't there; he was right beside us and we saw that the wheels were going to touch. From there on it was as if we were dreaming, as if we were lying in bed dreaming we were flying through the air upside down. After we first made contact with the wall, we don't remember anything till we woke up in the track hospital and wondered how the car was." I ask him how it's going at Pocono and he tells me that the first day out he was pretty cautious. "The second day we started running hard through the corners, but I noticed that we still weren't trying to prove anything in traffic. It takes a little

66

Billy Scott taping an interview in front
of his garage

while," he concludes. "It makes you realize you really could get hurt doing this kind of thing."

After Sneva's crash, the 500 began an anticlimactic slide toward a rain-shortened conclusion. Dallenbach, who had maintained his lead, dropped out thirty-six laps later, claiming his air intakes had gotten clogged with litter from the wreckage, causing him to burn a piston. Some drivers had other theories about what had caused the burned piston, but it was a sad end to what had been one of the most spectacular, come-from-behind drives in the history of the race.

The sky darkened radically, the wind began to whip up hot dog wrappers and dust devils in the infield, and within minutes the 500 had been transformed into a hydroplane race. The checkered and red flags appeared simultaneously and cars spumed rooster tails trying to make the start–finish line. There were multiple and relatively harmless spins and crashes, cars sliding, looping lazily down the straights, up the pit lane and through the corners. It was Bobby Unser's good fortune to be leading when the sky split open, and in a delicate ballet with his now tractionless tires, he crept toward the start–finish line. There were twenty-six more laps that would never be run and there would be seemingly endless theories and arguments by and for Rutherford and Foyt that had the race run its full course, they would have certainly won. It was the luck of the draw. It's made heroes and corpses without discretion.

Back in my motel room, I fix myself a drink and watch the rain pour down on the policemen channeling the postrace traffic on Sixteenth Street. I notice that the hair on the back of my arms has been singed; it balls and crumbles off like melted plastic. This whole month in Indianapolis seems like an abruptly ended dream. Two weeks from now, most of these drivers would be racing at Milwaukee, and it wouldn't much matter who had won today. The race had been important only because 400,000 paying spectators and millions more by their radios and TV sets had, by agreement, made it so. But now it was all over and another "agreement" was in force. The following day's sports section would carry the news that the Golden State Warriors had beaten the Washington Bullets for the National Basketball Association championship, and the cover of *Sports Illustrated* would carry a picture of Billy Martin, "Baseball's Fiery Genius." I have an autographed picture of the winner for my son, and I'm beginning to get drunk.

The next morning there's a photograph of Sneva's crash on the front page of the *Indianapolis Star*, and I recognize my own figure, fleeing ignominiously from the flames. On my way to the airport I drive past the Speedway, and all I can see is litter, two feet deep, in every visible tunnel, passageway and concourse, more than six million pounds of it. I stop for a red light and notice one more thing; the corpse of a huge tomcat lying next to the chain link fence. Someone has considerately propped its head up on a crushed beer can and crossed its paws in repose. *There's my story*, I thought. After twenty-five years of listening and dreaming, I've seen my first Indianapolis 500, and this is the one picture that will stick. Another great event chronicled in trash, another discarded container.

1976

I'm following Rick Muther's ancient, borrowed Barracuda down a winding Indiana country road toward the complex where he has taken an apartment for the month of May. Suddenly I realize we've fallen into a high-speed parade with a four-wheel-drive van leading Rick and another pickup truck joined in behind me. We're in a road race on a fairly tight course, each vehicle in turn diving on the apex of each bend in the road, dropping one front tire into the gravel, then sliding wide to the outside shoulder. It seems like old times. I had first met Muther over a decade earlier when he was racing sports cars in California. In fact, he was one of the first, non-Formula 1 road racers to break into the crew-cut, left-turn-only fraternity of Indy drivers. He has told me about a letter he received from then USAC president Henry Banks in 1968 suggesting he shave his mustache if he wanted to run at the Speedway. Muther complied. He shaved his mustache, but let his hair grow into the frizzy mane that has since become his trademark. Times were changing, and even tradition-bound Indianapolis had to make some concessions. If he was persistent, and had the necessary degree of skill, even a California hippie couldn't be kept out of the club.

I'm delighted with my pickup truck, which takes the corners smooth and flat. We're playing a game of mechanical horse, each trying in turn to duplicate the line of Mike Mosley, who I will discover is driving the van in the lead. Now we are winding through a maze of identical modern mansarded apartment buildings. Mosley slides his van to a stop in an empty carport and Muther, myself, and Mark Stainbrook, Rick's mechanic, park alongside. Muther introduces me to Mosley, and we go up to the apartment to have a few beers and to watch the rebroadcast of the second day's qualifying on television. Mosley is all smiles, like a kid who's just made a date with the homecoming queen. He's turned in the fastest time of the day, and third fastest overall, edging out Bobby Unser's time by seven hundredths of a second. He's a small, fairly delicate-looking man with steel-rimmed glasses and a sensitive, boyish grin, hardly fitting the mythical stereotype of the brawny, two-fisted Indy driver.

Muther and Mosley form perhaps the nucleus of the unofficial club of freaks among the drivers, mostly a new boys club which they identify as the "good guys" as opposed to the straights or "bad guys," the old school Indy drivers like Foyt, the Unsers, Andretti, etc., those who have come to be regarded here as "the establishment." Mosley, in beating out Unser's qualifying time, has scored a big one for the "good guys," though he'd be the last person to laud it as such.

"You beat Bobby Unser's speed by eight-eight hundredths of a mile an hour," says the track announcer, soliciting a victorious comment.

"Yup. That's pretty close," Mosley says, being characteristically modest and noncommittal.

"What's the secret? Where'd you get the extra speed?"

"I can't tell you," Mosley replies, his voice on the edge of jubilation. "That's why it's a secret."

The apartment, which Muther is sharing with Mark

Night before race ▶

Stainbrook, is spacious and fairly empty, a place to keep their clothes for the month of May, furnished only with black lights that give it a subdued, psychedelic atmosphere, and enormous pillows to lean back against while sitting on the floor. It's about as California as you can get on a modest budget in Indiana. Muther, Mosley, Mark and I are sitting crosslegged in a semicircle around the television set, waiting out *Hee Haw* for the taped report on the day's qualifying. Janet Guthrie has dominated the news for the past week, and though it seems like a tired question by now, I ask Rick if he thinks that if she were able to qualify, she would have the physical strength to drive the entire 500 miles.

"I don't know," he says, turning to gaze out the window at the last light of an overcast evening. "It's a crush for sure. I get pretty wrung out by it, but you do get a second wind in this race." Mosley nods in agreement. "After the first two hundred miles," Muther continues, "you think it's impossible, especially if it's hot. But then, all of a sudden you feel like you're starting fresh again and it seems almost easy."

We talk about the tension and the charged atmosphere of race day. A promo blurb for my article in the current *Playboy* describes Indy as the closest thing America has to rollerball. Muther comments on the description. "That's it all right. It's like three hundred thousand crazies drawn mysteriously to the same spot in the middle of America at the same time every year."

"Rollercar," Mosley interjects, "that's what we called it after we saw that movie." Mosley suffered two bad crashes at the Speedway in consecutive years, in 1971 and '72. He retired after winning last year's Milwaukee 200, but found that the quiet life he had sought back in California was too quiet, his bank account was suffering from lack of income, and all his friends were gone to the races. Most of the drivers agree, that he is a consistent charger who would be just about unbeatable in a really first-rate car.

I tell my story of standing on the inside of turn three with two motor-drive Nikons at the first false start of the 1973 race. I'm describing the unearthly sensation of watching, hearing and feeling those thirty-three cars go by with only a few feet of grass between me and them.

"I'll bet it would be," says Mosley. "I took a friend over to watch from the suites on turn two, and it's real scary there. It feels like you're gonna catch someone in your lap."

"I know," I nod in agreement, flashing on Sneva's airborne car hurtling toward me in flames.

"It's hard to believe how fast those cars come off that turn," he continues, "and some of them seem really bent outta shape. It looks a lot easier and solider for me looking from the inside out than it does from the outside in."

We have another round of beer and Muther and I reminisce a bit with some road-racing stories from the early sixties. "Did you ever want to drive here?" Mosley asks.

"Yeh, I did," I reply. "Sure, from as far back as I can remember. But coming here seemed quite a jump. It was always something almost mythical to me, so much different from any other race."

"It's different all right," Mosley laughs, and he and Muther exchange knowing grins.

74

"I was a pretty good driver at the kind of racing I did," I go on with my explanation, "I mean I won my fair share, but I never really knew if I was good enough to make it here."

"I guess you still don't know, do you?" Mosley smiles.

"No," I agree, "I guess that's something I'll never know." Mosley grins at Muther and then at me. He has tried it, and is better than just good enough. It's the grin of a man who knows.

Buck Owens and Roy Clark finish their last duet and it's time for the films of the day's qualifying. We're watching Foyt's rather disappointing run that put him in the middle of the second row—disappointing to A. J., that is. His car is loose, oversteering, the rear end coming out too easily on the corners. His first lap is a respectable 187 mph. His second falls to 186, his third to 184. On his final lap, his right rear tire kisses the wall coming out of turn four, an error that would have caused most drivers to lose it and probably write off their car as well, but when you see that kind of smoke from the tire and then the car bobbles slightly from the impact and straightens out, you know it's got to be A. J. Foyt, and you know that when he pulls off his helmet he's going to be wearing his mad mask.

"That was a pretty good run," says track announcer Del Clark, trying to keep an upbeat tone for the almost 150,000 race fans who pretty much expected A. J. to take the pole again for the third year in a row.

"It's a disgrace to me, my crew and my car," Foyt snaps back.

"Well what went wrong?" Clark asks, recovering from the momentary shock of A. J.'s bluntness, only to be blasted again.

"The damn thing wasn't handlin'. If you'd had your eyes open you coulda seen it for yourself."

"Did you hear that?" Mosley gasps, rolling backward with laughter. Both he and Muther are again amazed at the plain talk from Super Tex. It was all down on tape and no P.R. man had had a chance to launder it for public consumption. By now, however, that short fuse and lack of tact have become part of the Foyt legend.

It occurs to me that Muther and Mosley seem to have more fun out of racing; not that they don't take it seriously, but they seem to take themselves less seriously than the Unsers and the Foyts. They don't have a tough guy, almost legendary race-driver image to maintain. Though Muther is forty and Mosley twenty-nine, they project the impression of a couple of kids who are happy to be doing something they realize only a handful of people in the world are capable of doing, and happy to have been good enough and fortunate enough to have gotten away with it so far. As I sit here in front of the television set in this dimly lit room, I feel like I'm sitting with a couple of young World War I aces, ordinary men, except for what they are able to do with a race car, who are dedicated to taking life moment by moment as it comes.

John Martin is qualifying now, and though the television cameras and the subdued recorded sound make it seem almost leisurely, Muther is pointing out to me how Martin is diving down on the corners early, dropping a tire over the white line and pushing the car wide coming out, stretching the capabilities of his car to get the absolute maximum from it. "Martin's getting pretty damn good," Muther comments. Mosley nods in agreement. This is Martin's sixth year at the Speedway, and it frequently takes that long for a driver to begin to realize his full potential here. Several days before, I had heard Billy Vukovich say that for his first five years running here he felt completely lost, and that it was only after thousands and thousands of times around this two and a half miles of asphalt that he began to feel at home and to really get control of what he was doing.

Now Dick Simon is out, trying to qualify what Mosley and Muther consider to be an inferior handling car. "That thing just isn't going through the turns," Muther shakes his head. Still Simon is turning in laps in the 182 range.

"It's a banzai run," Mark exclaims, meaning an attempt made mostly on courage, a do-or-die effort to make an ill-handling car go around the track faster than it's really capable of going. Simon completes his fourth lap, and though we know we're watching him on video tape, we're relieved when it's over, and so is Dick Simon, relieved and delighted to have put his car in the middle of the sixth row, securely in the race.

I ask Rick and Mike what they do on race day mornings, what time they get up and head for the track. "Oh I don't like to get up too early," Muther says. "About nine, I guess."

"And you can still make it through the traffic?" I'm a little surprised. I have a nagging apprehension that I'm going to get caught up in a traffic sweep that will carry me irreversibly to Terre

Haute and funnel me down a dead-end, one-way street with a cop car sitting at the open end.

"Sure," Mosley chimes in, "the crush is pretty well over by ten o'clock."

"Don't you ever worry about not making it in time for the race?"

"I'll drive down sidewalks, over fields or anything I have to do to get there race day," Mosley says, and I get the impression that those kinds of maneuvers might help to alleviate the tension of the hours before the race. "It's sure a rush to see all those people though," he goes on. "It's like the whole world has turned out to judge your performance. Those grandstands just vibrate."

I tell them about being with a girl who was wearing a chartreuse Day-Glo blouse in the pits, and how when we walked past Johnny Rutherford, he stopped and said, "Ah, you're the girl in the first turn," which was where she had been watching practice and taking pictures that morning.

"Yeah, there's a spot there where it seems fairly slow," Muther nods.

"He probably spotted her on his warm-up laps," Mosley suggests. "I do that a lot. You're going slow and everybody's looking you over, but really, I'm down there peeking out of that cockpit, watching all those people, picking out faces in the crowd. Boy, it's a rush."

In 1953, Thomas W. Binford was an Indianapolis businessman who manufactured and distributed lubricants for heavy earth-moving equipment. He had no particular interest in auto racing, apart, that is, from the interest more or less imposed on anyone who lives in Indianapolis by their very proximity to the Speedway. But he was persuaded by several friends to chip in with them and rent a race car. They entered the car in the 1953 race. It practiced, but blew its engine the day before qualifying started, and lacking a spare, they towed it back to the garage and called it quits. Two years later, when the AAA, which had run the 500 since its inception, pulled out of racing in reaction to the horrible crash at Le Mans that killed over ninety spectators, a group of Indianapolis businessmen organized The United States Auto Club, to take over the 500 and to become the sanctioning body for championship racing. As a capable young executive, Binford was asked to serve on its board and was, at the age of thirty-two, elected president. Although he still did not feel really close to racing, he took it on as a civic responsibility and served until 1969.

"I don't know how I got to be Chief Steward of this race," he says, pausing to light his pipe. "I think I have Ray Marquette of the *Indianapolis Star* to thank for that. When Harlen Fengler resigned, Marquette ran a headline that read, *Binford to Be Chief Steward?* That was the first I knew about it, though I guess he'd checked it out with the Speedway management and they'd already made the decision." Not that Binford really needed the additional responsibility

to fill up his already spare time. He was chief executive officer of the largest bank in Indiana, president of DePauw University and organizer and part owner of the newly formed Indiana Pacers basketball team.

Fengler had resigned after the 1973 race amid a great deal of controversy about his competence and his sometimes dogmatic and autocratic methods. "I don't think all the charges made against Harlen were justified, but he'd become defensive and had gotten a lot of bad press. Anyway, when I took over I had to create a discipline, overcome a nice-guy image I'd had." He lights his pipe again, watching the flame through his dark-lensed, tortoise-shell sunglasses. He's a compact, well-built man who, now in his mid-fifties, radiates competence and an almost total absence of self-importance. We are sitting in a rather bare concrete room under the grandstands along the main straightaway which serves as his working office at the Speedway. There is one ancient steel desk and two metal chairs of the same vintage. We can hear the muted sounds of racers diving into turn one, trying to get up speed for the upcoming first day of qualifying.

"I had never been a race official before, and suddenly here I was, Chief Steward. Well, I was pretty nervous that first year. I mean, racing is a hobby for no one. It's not like officiating a football game or a basketball game. You can never be frivolous about it. There are lives on the line. There's that presence of death that makes it different, intensifies everything, but also there's a spirit of adventure about it that's getting hard to find in our everyday life. Anyway, that first year was tough for me, and there was that decision about Johnny Rutherford that made me unpopular with Rutherford and his crew and probably some of his fans as well."

I hadn't attended the 1974 race and asked him to explain that decision to me.

"Well the rules state that in order to be assured a chance to make a qualifying run on the first day, and thus to have a chance at the pole, a car must be continuously in line in the position its owners have drawn in the qualifying order. Well, Rutherford's crew removed his car to the garage for half an hour to do some work on it, and I ruled that they must thereby forfeit their place in line. It was a tough decision to make and it cost Rutherford his chance to run for the pole, but I figured if I stuck to the rules with a Rutherford or a Foyt, I wouldn't have any trouble enforcing them with a Salt Walther or a Boom-Boom Cannon. Well, as you can imagine, Rutherford was furious about it. Fortunately, he won the race that year, and he couldn't continue to be mad at anyone. But for me it was just a matter of the rules."

I asked him if he didn't think some of the rules governing the race were a little outdated.

"The rules don't have anything to do with right or wrong," Binford laughs. He's about to explain when he gets a call over his walkie-talkie, which keeps him constantly available for consultation. He answers a few questions concerning a driver's credentials and relights his pipe. Shim Malone, the Assistant Chief Steward, brings in a form for Binford to sign, officially certifying that Billy Scott has successfully completed his refresher test. "A pretty consistent job," Binford says, looking over the lap times.

"He looked pretty good," Malone agrees.

"As I was saying," Binford continues, "the rules don't have

much to do with reason. They don't even have to make sense. They're just the agreements under which we run this race. Some of them, I'm sure, are pretty outmoded, but they're tradition, and tradition is the glue that holds this race together. Tradition itself answers a lot of questions, but it's a two-edged sword. I can't see for the life of me, for example, why we start this race with three cars abreast. Every other race is started with two cars abreast. It makes imminent good sense, but I can't get anyone to listen to me when I suggest changing it. There are a lot of things like that."

I begin to feel the pressures that must be crowding in on his time. I tell him that I'm aware he has many people making demands on him, and I don't want to monopolize his afternoon, but he puts me at ease. "They can reach me if they need me." He smiles, holding up his walkie-talkie.

"You were talking about tradition," I say, leading him back to his narrative.

"Everything gets magnified here." He rests his elbows on the desk and leans toward me for emphasis. "It's the richest race in the world, the most dangerous, and most of the famous drivers spend an entire month here every year. In fact, we've got so much time here that every little thing gets chewed over and we've got to be careful they don't get magnified out of proportion. We've got journalists, as you know, who have to spend a month here too, and if there isn't some kind of controversy, they almost have to create one to keep the interest up."

"Has your own interest in racing increased since you've become Chief Steward?" It's hard for me to imagine how someone

SEC
46

Guards watching first cars coming
in at dawn

The new look in gate guards at the Indianapolis Motor Speedway

could have taken on this demanding and rather thankless job—
which requires him to deal with some very egocentric racing drivers,
crew chiefs, car owners and lesser officials, some of whom have
held their jobs since the days when the race was run with riding
mechanics aboard most of the cars—if he didn't have an almost
consuming passion for the sport. But before I've finished the
question, I realize that those difficulties and complexities, that
intricate network of egos and mindless tradition are the very
elements that would make this job attractive to a man like Tom
Binford.

"Oh yes. I've had to become interested in it. The intensity of
my involvement here almost demands it." He pauses to light his
pipe again. "There are a lot of races I enjoy watching more, but this
is always *the* race. Nurburgring is impressive and they get 220,000
spectators there, but they're all spread out. Here, you can't help but
feel intimidated on race day. I look at all those people and realize
that nobody could control them; nobody could run this race. You
almost get the feeling that if all the officials went away, the race
would run itself."

I clear my throat and reposition myself on the straight-
backed chair. I don't know why I should feel uncomfortable asking
him about Janet Guthrie; I suppose it's because she's gotten so
much attention and so much publicity that any question about her
has already begun to sound like a cliché.

"I think it's great we've got a woman trying to make this
race. I think it's probably overdue, and I'm glad it's someone who's
really qualified and sincere about her effort rather than someone
just trying to make a point, to just break down barriers."

"Some of the other drivers don't seem to be thrilled about
her being here," I say, recalling conversations in Gasoline Alley and
some graffiti, "Janet Guthrie, Nookie of the Year," on the wall of
the men's room behind the pits.

Race Day morning on 16th Street

Binford leans back in his chair and scratches his head. "Obviously, she's getting some breaks here because she's a woman, but everybody gets breaks, one way or another. I think those drivers who complain the most about her being here are the ones who feel most threatened by her presence, drivers who've gotten some breaks here because of who they were. They've all proven themselves." He holds up his hands. "Don't get me wrong, but you know that a Billy Vukovich or a Gary Bettenhausen wouldn't have gotten their first rides here as easily as they did if their names had been Binford or Gerber." His pipe has gone out again, and he gives up on it and lights a cigarette.

"I think it's too bad she doesn't have a better car and that there has to be so much pressure on her. It's tough enough being a rookie here without all the attention from the media.'"

"The last two races here, since you've taken over as Chief Steward, have been remarkably safe." I'm trying to soften what has to sound like a pretty blunt question, but he's not going to wait for me to ask it.

"I like to think I've done everything I could to make them safe, made improvements in the track and spectator areas, the pacer light system, tried to foster a discipline among the drivers, but I realize that just plain luck has had a lot to do with it. Sooner or later, that record will get tarnished. I'm horrified when there's an accident, just like anybody else, but I've got a job, something I have to do. I can't justify racing. You either like it or you don't. It's just the way it is."

Tony Hulman is having problems with his Cadillac Seville. Each time he puts it in gear, it stalls. He doesn't seem to be flustered by it. He sits erectly behind the wheel and starts it again. "I don't know what the problem is," he says in a very quiet voice, turning to glance over his shoulder at me. "You all right back there? I'm sorry about the mess." The front passenger seat and half the back is piled high with books, pictures, luggage and a breathing machine he uses to alleviate his emphysema. He had cleared a space for me by piling some of this paraphernalia to the left. I'm holding a marble pen holder on my lap. It bears a plaque recognizing his thirty years as head man at the Speedway. Finally, he's tricked the balky fuel system and has the car moving. We drive away from the Speedway office behind the pits and head for the new office building and museum just inside the southeast turn. I notice how every official, gate guard and traffic controller, most of whom seem to be old men, recognizes this black Cadillac and seems to nod and wave respectfully as it passes. It's as if Hulman were *El Patron* in this separate empire within the Speedway gates.

We stop at the infield hospital so that he can have the doctor check over his breathing machine. He shows me around and points out with pride that this hospital could, in a pinch, serve the emergency needs of a city of 350,000 people, which, in effect, on race day, it does. He pauses to interview a young doctor, new to

92

the Speedway. The intern has just graduated from the University of Iowa, and Mr. Hulman shakes his hand and warmly welcomes him to Indiana. The intern seems as grateful for the recognition as if he'd just been officially certified by the Indiana State Medical Board, and I can understand his reaction. This mild-mannered, handsome still almost athletic-looking man of seventy-five is the voice I've heard on the radio every Memorial Day I can remember, exhorting the "Gentlemen" to start their engines. I don't know how it was for my contemporaries in New York or California or Iowa, but in one small town in Michigan the sound of those words represented the most intensely exciting moment of the year.

Tony Hulman is just settling into his office in the new Museum Building. It's a very large room with a long conference table. He hasn't yet organized his pictures, books and the plethora of service award plaques piled on the long credenza behind his desk. I take a seat in one of the leather upholstered chairs in front of his desk, and after scanning a few pieces of mail, he comes from behind the desk and takes the other chair to my right. It's a democratic gesture removing the formal expanse of rosewood between us.

I ask him when he first became interested in auto racing, and he tells me that he was never particularly interested in it. "Golf was my sport," he says, nodding toward the nine fairways in the infield of the Speedway, "golf and deep sea fishing. I used to see

this race sometimes, because it was a local event, but mostly I would listen to it on the radio while I was playing golf." He went to Yale and then came back to Terre Haute to work for the family wholesale merchandise company. "I sold and promoted our Clabber Girl Baking Powder from 1928 till after the war when the ready mixes came in." He smiles. "They sort of took the juice out of the baking powder business. And I did a lot of deep sea fishing too; that was really my sport back then. I was captain of the U.S. Tuna Team until 1952."

   "What about the Speedway?" I ask, trying to tie it in with baking powder and tuna fishing.

   "Well, the Speedway got pretty run-down during the war, and Eddie Rickenbacker decided to dispose of it. Wilbur Shaw had been looking around and thought about getting a number of companies interested, but"—he pauses to light a cigarette and looks at the ceiling as he continues—"he decided he didn't want eight or ten bosses. I wasn't a rabid race fan at that time, but I thought maybe it'd be worth taking a chance on. So I bought the track and put Wilbur Shaw in as president, and he ran it till 1954 when he had that plane crash coming back from Detroit." He puts his left hand in the pocket of his suitcoat and looks at the ceiling again as he takes a long drag on his cigarette. He takes a moment to sort out his memories, then seems to hit on the one he's

been looking for. "We had a hard time getting the track ready for the 1946 race. The grandstands were run-down. We put up what now seem small grandstands, and I wondered how we'd ever fill 'em. Wilbur was afraid of fire; the grandstands were wooden then, you know. So we used to wet them down with a fire hose every night, and we were always afraid they might collapse.

"We wondered if anyone would come, but we found that people had lined up the night before, and some of them couldn't get in before the race was over. I must have gotten a thousand letters about that. But we just couldn't handle the traffic." He seems to be enjoying the reminiscence. "I always remember"— he puts his hand on my arm for emphasis—"there was an article in the San Francisco newspaper about how lucky Captain Rickenbacker had been to find a couple of Hoosiers," he draws out the "ooo" sound and laughs to himself as he does, "to take that white elephant off his hands."

I'd often wondered about the term, Hoosier, and ask him if he knows its origin.

"I don't know where it comes from," he says with a slightly bewildered smile. "I've always been one, but I've never been able to find out what it means." He clears his throat and continues his story. "Everybody said, Why would anybody want to watch a car go one hundred miles an hour when boys were flying airplanes at five hundred or six hundred miles an hour? Well, race day came, and I got caught up in traffic, clear over on the other side of town and almost missed the race. I had no idea where all those people were going. It didn't occur to me that they could all be going to the track. Anyway, Wilbur and I had to get out and run, down sidewalks, through fields, and barely got here, all soaked with perspiration."

I tell him that all that must seem like ancient history now, and he nods and looks out the window at a car flashing through the southeast turn. "I think about everything's changed here except the track. The old roadsters got pretty unsteady on those bricks. Jack Brabham talked to me about it in 1962 when he came here with the first rear-engined car, and so we thought we'd pave it and make it safer. But we didn't want to change the slope or the configuration. We wanted that to remain as a constant. We've seen the development of the automobile around this track, you know, and the speeds here have always sort of been a yardstick." He leans toward me, smiles and touches my arm again. "If somebody had told Pete DePaolo back in 1925 when he won the race at about one hundred miles an hour that there'd be cars going one hundred and eighty to two hundred miles an hour here, he'd have told 'em to go look for a psychiatrist."

It's getting late, and I thank him for taking the time to talk to me. "Oh, thank you," he says, "I'm delighted that you want to come down here and write about all this." He insists on giving me a ride back to the pits.

As we're walking toward his car, we are stopped by an old man in a Speedway Safety Patrol uniform. "Have you heard where we'll be working this year Mr. Hulman?"

Tony is taken by surprise and at a loss for an answer. "Oh, um, I don't know." He's struggling to be gracious. "Have you

asked Clarence?" (He's referring to Clarence Cagle, the superintendent of grounds.)

"He hasn't made up his mind yet." The old man sighs and it occurs to me that this "old man" is probably at least ten years younger than Tony Hulman.

"Well, good to see you," Tony says, taking the man's hand.

"Thank you, Tony," the man says reverently, making a small bow. He opens the car door for Tony and waves again as we drive away.

Janet Guthrie is walking down the concrete alley that separates the tower grandstands from the garage area. It's a rare moment when she finds herself alone. She's been the biggest news at the Speedway this year and has generated at least a 25 percent increase in prerace publicity, not because she's the hottest rookie in recent memory, or because she's one of the half-dozen drivers who actually might win this race, but simply because she's a woman.

Four years ago, women weren't even allowed in the pits or in the garage area. It was quite a shock to the traditionalists when the restrictions were lifted in 1973, permitting wives and girl friends of the drivers and even female journalists to walk on this ground that had theretofore been sanctified exclusively for male soles. But equal opportunity laws had to come, even to Indianapolis, and this year, for the first time, you might find a driver or a mechanic flirting with one of the gate guards. And most of them would probably even admit that they find these young women in hard hats and well-fitting Levis a definite improvement over the old-timers, some of whom have been manning their posts for so many years they seem to have become part of the facility.

But a woman in a driver's suit—I mean, a woman actually out there in a racing car on the same track with the A. J. Foyts and Bobby Unsers—that's something that the yardbirds, those denizens with grooves in their elbows from leaning against the infield fences, can't quite bring themselves to accept. There are all the other drivers, and then there's Janet. When she goes out on the track, they all crowd the fences to get a glimpse of her blue McLaran flashing by, and try to convince themselves that there's actually a woman driving that car, a woman just like their mothers or their wives or their sisters. But she's not like their sisters or their wives or their "sainted mothers," no more than they are like A. J. Foyt or Johnny Rutherford. This woman happens to be a racing driver with thirteen years of experience and, in her own mind at least, she's come here like any other rookie to try and qualify for the biggest auto race in the world.

It's tough enough being an ordinary rookie at Indianapolis. It's a scary track, sometimes even for drivers who've driven the 500 a dozen times or more; there are so many tricks to learn, so many quirks about its four totally individual turns that can keep a new driver from getting up to speed or can put him into the wall.

And a rookie is under constant scrutiny. He has to prove himself to the veteran drivers and to the army of technical observers who are watching him every moment, trying to pick out flaws or inconsistencies in his driving, any imperfection that might indicate that he isn't quite good enough to be allowed a chance to try and qualify. But for Janet Guthrie, that's only half the pressure she has to contend with. She's big news, and if I want to find her at any moment, all I have to do is look for the paparazzi, that cloud of photographers, reporters and TV crews that hound her constantly. It's news every time she puts on her driving suit or goes to the ladies' room. She's being photographed every moment she's at the Speedway, and I'm certain that if a photographer could catch her picking her nose, it'd make the front page of the sports section.

Though some of them may resent her being here, most of the drivers, crews, officials and spectators are at least polite to her. Oh, there are a few catcalls and whistles when her name is spoken over the public address system, and privately some of the drivers grumble about her getting a ride "just because she's a woman." But most of them will admit that if she had a better car, she'd stand a pretty good chance of getting it in the race, and when the airlines lost her luggage, Billy Vukovich loaned her his driving suit so she could practice and get ready to take her rookie test. And she feels she's been treated fairly. She just wishes the press would leave her alone so she could concentrate on her driving.

But on this particular morning, as she is walking to the Speedway press room to meet me for yet another interview, she is stopped by two slightly beer-crazed twenty-year-olds. "Hey Janet," one of them calls, "you gonna qualify?"

"I hope so," she replies, smiling, perhaps a little nervously.

"Well we don't," the other boy calls back to her. "We hope you crash and burn where we can see you."

She is obviously a little shaken by the encounter. Race drivers do sometimes crash and burn, but they don't talk much or speculate about it, and they'd like to think that that's not the reason all those people come here to watch them.

"That's really the only bad treatment I've experienced since I've been here," she tells me. She has a disarmingly sweet smile and a definite feminine air about her, not at all the butch sort of toughness I'd preconceived about any woman who would try to compete in this most difficult and dangerous of all sporting events.

There is no doubt in her own mind that she would be able to drive the entire five hundred miles if she should be able to qualify. "I've proven that lots of times in twelve- and twenty-four-hour races." I can tell she's a little tired of having her strength brought into question. I tell her that some of the other drivers have complained of sore necks and shoulders from the time they've spent practicing. "Well they must be out of shape then," she replies, "because I feel just fine."

Paula Murphy, the world's record holder among female drag racers, has been in town and has made some comments in the local papers that while she thinks women can compete in drag races and road races, she feels they have no place on the

**The Purdue Golden Girl entertains early ▶
arrivals on the front straight**

superspeedways, that they simply aren't strong enough. At the mention of Paula Murphy's name, Janet hisses. I laugh. "I read that," she explains, "and she came by to tell me she really didn't mean all that, and to wish me well, sort of in spite of my being a woman, but what does she know? She's a drag racer. They only have to drive for six or eight seconds."

"The rookie test was no problem," she goes on. "I was confident I could do that. I'd pretty well established that at Trenton. But when we try getting up to qualifying speeds, that's when it'll get tough."

"Have you had any flashes about what you're doing?" I ask. "I mean, have you had any trouble bringing yourself to realize that you're really driving at Indianapolis?"

"I've been so busy." She takes a deep breath, blows it out and blinks her eyes several times rapidly, as if she were, just this moment, trying to sort it all out. "I haven't had much time to think about it being Indianapolis. Only, at a few odd moments, I've looked up and seen that Gasoline Alley sign." She seems to relax a bit, and I get the feeling that, for the first time, she's not regarding me as an adversary.

"I first came here in February when it was all deserted and the trees were bare, and there was nobody here but some birds," she explains. "I remember watching two doves soaring up and perching on the top of the grandstands. It was so quiet, it was almost spooky. I tried to imagine the leaves coming out and the stands filling up with people. I've been warned about the effect it can have on you, seeing all those people and realizing they're looking at you."

"What about the wall?" I ask. I know that some highly skilled road racers, like Chris Amon, haven't been able to cope with it whistling by at two hundred miles an hour, a few inches from their right ears, and most drivers say they never really get used to it.

"It's definitely a concern." Janet flattens her palm out above the table, and her eyes open wide. "I've encountered walls before, at Daytona and at Trenton, but they were never going by quite this fast. I haven't really been up to it yet; till I work up to qualifying speeds, I guess I won't really know till then. But, my biggest concern has been in the pits." She laughs.

"In the pits?" I ask, wondering what she could be talking about.

"Yeah, to keep from running over all those photographers."

It's the Happy Hour, that period between five o'clock and the six o'clock closing on practice days when the track is usually reserved for veteran drivers. The Happy Hour is another sometime practice that has become one of those unwritten rules Tom Binford talked about. Late in the afternoon, the wind usually dies down, the air is a bit cooler and the turbocharged engines can operate at peak efficiency. It's the time the hot shoes usually choose to wring it out and turn in some fast prequalifying times that might psyche their competitors. There's no rule that says that rookies can't be running then, but if the track is fast and crowded, the officials will usually pull them in. And that's what's happened to Janet Guthrie on this particular Friday afternoon, the last day before the first weekend of time trials. All week she's been plagued with mechanical difficulties and now, just as she's ready to complete the final phase of her rookie test, twenty laps at any speed over 165, A. J. Foyt, Gordon Johncock and Tom Sneva come screaming down the front straight, pushing their lap speeds to the upper 180s, and Shim Malone decides it's no time for rookies to be learning their way around.

I'm sitting on the pit wall, talking with a P.R. man from a small Indiana college. He's here shooting some footage of the activities for his college's UHF television station. Our conversation is interrupted as A. J. passes again, the scream of his Ford Coyote suffusing our words. We both turn and glance at the red blur as his car fades into the first turn and feel that slightly prickly sensation you get hearing that V8 wound to its maximum, knowing he's pushing the car just a little farther than it can comfortably go. It's quiet again now, but we've forgotten what we were talking about.

"I don't care about being here for the race," he says, and though I think I know what he's saying, I ask him why. "I haven't come since '73," he says, rubbing his arms as if they were cold. "There's just too much tension, that and the boredom. On race day I always feel like I'm about to lose my lunch."

Phyllis Diller and notables in race parade

The Race Queen

"I know what you mean," I tell him.

He nods and looks up and down the length of the empty grandstands across the track. "A lot of people who aren't race fans come to this race. They're Indy fans. It just seems so much more dramatic than other races, I almost want to go hide somewhere till it's over." I nod. "Maybe I'll come back and watch it this year." He looks down at the pavement, considering what he's said. "But I doubt it," he adds as A. J.'s Coyote screams past again.

Jerry Sneva, Tom Sneva's younger brother, is hanging around Gasoline Alley, looking for a ride. "It'll be easier finding one next week," he says, "after the first weekend of time trials. There'll be cars that haven't gotten up to speed by then, and owners will be gettin' in a panic, lookin' for any change that might help 'em make the race."

"That's kind of a tough way to try and make it, isn't it?" I ask him. "I mean, with a car that some other driver hasn't been able to do anything with."

"Sure it is." He raises his eyebrows in a comic gesture and stiffens up momentarily, like a toy soldier. "But," he adds, "if you can make it go, people pay a lot more attention." He makes a gesture with his hands as if he were holding a steering wheel, sawing it back and forth. "On the other hand"—he pauses to bite his lower lip—"if you go slower, that's not so good, 'cause they notice that too. You've just got to put your foot in it," he says, making the steering gesture again, wiggling his hips as he does. "That's what it's all about."

I wonder if Indianapolis is anything like this in, say, February or July. I tend to think of it, apart from May, as a fairly conservative midwestern city, distinguished by its two gigantic war memorials, a plethora of banks and financial institutions (Wall Street on the Wabash) and as the birthplace of a writer named Vonnegut, a name still seen on several hardware stores. But this evening, as I'm driving from the Speedway toward downtown to meet some friends for dinner at St. Elmo's Steakhouse, it seems more like Los Angeles or maybe even Tralfamador.

I'd seen a lot of weirdness here, but most of it in and around the Speedway. There were the Thursday night amateur topless go-go contests at Mother Tucker's, which more often than not became bottomless as well, local ladies of the night gyrating in every imaginable posture in a desperate effort to outgross the competition for the loudest applause and a cash prize. Those were things I'd more or less sought out. But on this particular evening

I don't even have to look for it. It comes to me as if my air-conditioned car were a sealed space capsule traveling through some sort of an X-rated Disneyworld.

I've just crossed the White River and am passing a used car lot when I notice someone standing on top of a car. As I get closer, I can see the person is wearing a bikini and red terry-cloth booties, and that she's dancing on the car roof to attract patrons to *The Aloha Club Topless Dancers*. It's kind of like some hamburger stands where they have a clown out front to beckon customers in off the street, except this silent barker had a special trick that I rather egocentrically assume is intended just for me. As I'm just a few yards short of the Aloha, she turns away from me, pulls down her bikini bottom and flashes two melon-shaped globes at me, so dazzlingly white that for several seconds I see spots before my eyes as if I'd just been shot, point-blank with a flash gun. I turn down Meridian, still blinking and trying to refocus my vision when I pass a parking lot in which I notice two men circling one another. Again, the timing is perfect. Just as I'm in position to see them clearly, one man punches the other in the jaw. The strikee falls backward, his head bouncing off the pavement like a semideflated basketball. The striker then begins to drop-kick him in the ribs, but my view becomes obscured by a parked car. A third man is standing by with his hands in his pockets, more as if he were watching a crap game than a street brawl. I'm surprised that I'm not disturbed or startled by these passing vignettes. I tell myself that they probably have nothing to do with the race, but after a couple of weeks here in the month of May, they just seem like part of the big show, and I wouldn't be surprised to learn that the two men in the parking lot were fighting over the usable horsepower of the Drake Offy as against that of a Cosworth Ford.

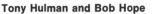

Billy Scott is back this year with a better car, one that might actually make the race. I'm talking with him in the pits between practice runs when Larry McCoy, a second-year Indy driver, stops and asks him what kind of times he's getting.

"Mid 170s," Scott says, shrugging his shoulders.

"Same as everybody else." McCoy nods his head and stands with his hands on his hips looking over Scott's car.

"Yep."

"You holding your breath yet?" McCoy grins.

"Not yet." Scott looks at McCoy as if to say, *Are you crazy?* "It's too early for me to be holding my breath. I don't have a back-up car."

"Well, we're getting 180s," McCoy says, matter-of-factly.

"You holdin' *your* breath yet?" Scott glances at him sideways, so as not to seem too interested in his response.

"I had sore lungs last night, literally," McCoy says, and they laugh away the tension between them.

Another driver is hanging around the pits, wearing his driving suit long after his car has been towed back to the garage, and Scott looks at him disdainfully. "He probably wears it when he goes out at night to make sure everybody knows he's a driver."

"He's a rookie," I say. "He's excited."

Billy wrinkles up his face in an exaggerated smile and then lets it go slack. "Big deal," he says.

Tony Hulman and Bob Hope

In the last few minutes of practice before the qualifying begins, I hear over the P.A. system that Billy has been involved in an accident. Then I hear him being praised for his evasive action in missing Spike Gehlhausen, another rookie who hit the wall in turn one, shedding three wheels across the track in front of him. Scott dove to the inside to avoid the wheels and spun on the grass inside the short chute. I find him in the pits near the tower where he's just been interviewed by the track announcer.

"Boy it was really neat," he tells me as we walk back toward the garage, "just like in the movies, stuff flyin' off that car, comin' around me and past me, and I'm goin' right through it. The only bad part of it is though"—he makes a face as if he'd just smelled something—"we probably flattened out our tires, and it's the only set we've got scrubbed in to qualify on."

Gordon Johncock stops Billy to tell him that with all the delays in getting qualifying started, he'll probably have time to scrub in new tires before his number comes up. It's a magnanimous gesture from a veteran toward a rookie. "I didn't mean to spin," Scott explains to Johncock, "but as soon as I hit the grass, it was adios."

One of Bignotti's crewmen hollers at him as we pass, "Ya change your drivin' suit yet Billy?"

"Naw, nothin' like that," he replies. His manner is that of a kid who has just pulled off a new trick on his dirt bike. His tires are dirty and flat-spotted badly, but he can't move his car out of

line without losing his chance to qualify. Fortunately, the track closes before his number comes up, so he'll have time to scrub in a new set in the practice period the following morning.

His best time so far has been 177 mph. The next afternoon in a qualifying attempt, he turns three laps consistently at 178 and change, but Jim Wright, his crew chief, waves off the attempt as he feels it might not be good enough to make the race. When he pulls in, Scott complains that he doesn't like the way the car's handling, that it's getting loose in the turns. His crew changes the angle of the wing, and adjusts the crossweight. A Goodyear technical adviser checks the temperatures, measures the circumference of the tires and his crew puts an extra one-eighth inch of bump rubber on the right-rear shock to alleviate the pushing coming out of the turns, but the track closes before he has another chance to qualify. "Well it gives us another week to see what kind of speed we can get up to," he says. "I'd rather worry about that than about somebody else bumping us if we had taken that 178."

During the five days before the second weekend of time trials, he manages to get his speed up to the high 179s, still not fast enough to be sure about qualifying. But just before noon on Friday, he has what will turn out to be a bit of racing luck; he blows the last engine he has and is forced to call his sponsor, Warner Hodgdon in San Bernardino, to ask if he can buy a new one.

"Are there any available?" Hodgdon asks.

"Vels-Parnelli's got one for fifteen thousand," Billy says, a little tentatively.

"Buy it," Hodgdon says.

Scott took the new engine out to warm it up in practice Saturday morning. "The first time I stood on it, I knew it was the best engine we'd ever had," he says, "but we didn't get a chance to turn any hot laps to see what kind of times we could get with it." About five o'clock in the afternoon, he got his chance to try it out when he took the green flag from Pat Vidan at the start of his qualifying run. "On the first lap I knew I was going fast, but I had no idea we were turning a 184.6. I wasn't even holding my breath. We waited till late in the afternoon when there was nobody waitin' in line so we didn't have to wait around and think about it. We couldn't decide whether we ought to refuel and scuff up the tires.

"I went out and ran one lap. When I came in, Jim just said, 'You turned a 181.8. Get in line.' We checked the fuel and found we had just enough to qualify with if we didn't take more than one warm-up lap. We got in line. They checked the wing height, inserted the pop-off valve, cleared the track and I took off. I mean I was really pumped up and ready to go. I was pushin' it, but it seemed almost easy. I mean I didn't even have to hold my breath." I thought about how different it must seem when everything is working for a driver, different from the banzai run of Dick Simon who must have been holding his breath the whole four laps. "We finally had it dialed in, and I knew we were going to make the show." He pauses a minute to catch his breath and to let his story catch up with him. "Jim didn't signal me any speed. He just gave me a plus sign to let me know I was going fast enough. If

he'd of signaled me a 184.6, I'd probably have been so startled
I'd have dropped down to a 150 on the next lap."

    As it was, he only dropped to a 183, and maintained an
average of 183.383, making him the fastest rookie in the field,
edging out Vern Schuppan by 1.5 seconds for the ten-mile run.
"Hey, I got fifteen hundred dollars and a trophy," he tells me. He's
a kid who has gotten what he always wanted for Christmas. "Of
course the money won't last long," he shrugs, "but that trophy'll
be nice to have." He puts his hand on my shoulder. "There aren't
many people who have a trophy from Indy."

    I drive him back to the apartment he's taken with his crew.
We stop at a 24-hour grocery, and he buys a bottle of Pepsi and
a box of animal crackers. He opens the box of crackers and begins
munching them as we get back in my truck. "Sunday's my day."
He stretches with excitement. "I don't want to sleep too late.
Sometimes I wake up at two in the morning, and I've had a
nightmare that I've missed the race. I want to be there for all the
parades and pageantry."

    "It sounds like you're excited," I laugh.

    "Is a frog waterproof?" He rocks forward in the cab of the
truck, then rolls back, crosses his legs, then uncrosses them as
if he didn't know what to do with himself to pass the time until
race day.

Heavy traffic in turn

The start of the race, from turn one

Swede Savage crashes exiting turn four — 1973

Losing to the odds at Indy

(Left) Emergency crew extinguishes the fire following Tom Sneva's spectacular flip in turn two **(Below)** Fire extinguishers along the pit wall

The wreckage of Tom Sneva's car on the grass inside turn two

(Above) The turbo charger "pop-off" valve
(Right) A. J. Foyt's crew pushes him
back toward the track

Johnny Rutherford underway after a pit stop

(Below left) Rutherford's crew constructs a makeshift tent to keep the rain off while waiting for the restart that never came

Johnny Rutherford ready for the start of the 1976 race

**Winner Bobby Unser and car owner Dan Gurney in
Victory Lane following the rain-shortened 1975 race**

In 1971, Rick Muther was following David Hobbs out of turn four when Hobbs suddenly lost power. Muther swerved to the left to miss Hobbs, hit the inside wall twice and careened back across the track into the outside wall. As Muther's car collapsed around him Hobbs, who had fallen behind the carnage, hit him broadside, tilting him up on two wheels and sending him skidding sideways down the front straight like a Joey Chitwood stunt driver. "I was lucky that time." Muther smiles and rolls his eyes toward the sky. "We were running aluminum wheels instead of magnesium; otherwise they'd of caught fire for sure." As it was, he came out of it with a broken sternum and dashed hopes.

This year his luck has been less spectacular but nevertheless bad. No thrill ride for the spectators on the main straight; in fact, no ride at all. His car owner had burned up two engines, testing in California, and arrived at the Speedway a week late. "I don't know, señor," Muther says, shaking his head. He lets all the air out so that his shoulders almost seem to collapse on his navel. "He used bearings people stopped using four or five years ago. I guess he got a good deal on 'em, I don't know. We didn't get a good crankshaft till the night before the last day of qualifying. I drove out to the airport to pick it up and Mark and I stayed up all night to get it in, but we didn't have time to run a block leak test. We started it up the next morning, and there was water in the cylinders. The block was cracked, and there isn't much you can do about that."

It's the following Thursday now, three days before the race, and Rick is getting ready to leave for the airport to catch his plane back to California. "You've just gotta come here prepared," he tells me, "A month seems like a long time, but you gotta be ready to race when you get here." In his flowered Hawaiian shirt he slumps on a toolbox and looks at the immaculate but nonfunctional blue and yellow Eagle that won't get past the pit gates again this year. "When I started out in this game I was going to be rich and famous, señor. Now I've got to go back home and start all over again, tryin' to scratch up a sponsor. Well, at least I've still got my arms and legs, and no bad burns." He sighs. "At least I'm still pretty."

"I wish you were going to stick around for the race," I tell him.

"I can't." He shakes his head and slides on his mirror-finished sunglasses, as if they'd filter out all the reminders of his disappointment. "This place makes me sad if I'm not in the show. It's just too intense to watch from behind the fence. I'll be on the beach Sunday, señor. He smiles. "Maybe I'll listen to it on the radio. Maybe I'll be ridin' a wave."

Later that afternoon, I'm sitting with Mike Mosley on the wall that separates the pits from the track, watching the final moments of pit-stop practice. It's a pleasant sunny afternoon, the grandstands across the track are empty, and there's a deceptively low-key atmosphere. The ABC-TV crew is filming some practice pit-stops for their delayed broadcast of the race, and the buses that take museum visitors around the Speedway are running again for the first time since the track opened three weeks ago. One stops behind us while the driver explains what's going on in the pits, and we turn and wave at the faces behind glass—

like mechanical figures in a Disneyland Raceworld. We are talking
about the drivers' meeting, which is due to start in a few minutes.
I tell Mike about having snuck into the meeting last year and
ask him if he feels the drivers really do heed Tom Binford's
exhortation about the start, not to begin racing till they come out
of the second turn.

"I don't know," he says, glancing over the Tower Terrace
stands, "It's pretty wild out there the first few laps. When they're
over you kind of settle down, and it's all right."

"Does being three abreast add to it?" I ask.

"Yeah, here it does, 'cause it's so narrow. There's no room
if anybody makes a mistake. I don't like it much, to tell you the
truth." He laughs. "In fact, I don't like it at all. They clean the
track, but there's still a lot of sand and you can't see very well.
You have to wear three or four face shields to rip off as they get
dirty, and each one of them distorts things a little more. I just
hope everyone keeps it together and doesn't try to win it on the
first lap."

The sound of the impact wrenches fades, and the last car
is wheeled from the pit lane. A few crews are still working on their
refueling tanks. A lady with a really outstanding décolletage walks
past, and we are both silent in a moment of admiration.

Mike Mosley

T hat evening, we are back in Mark Stainbrook's apartment in Clermont where I first met Mosley. We are all feeling Rick Muther's conspicuous absence and listening to a new Charlie Daniels Band record, *Saddle Tramp*. Mike breaks our rather melancholy trance by lamenting that he can't have music in his racing car.

"If you could work it out," I suggest, "you'd have to program your tapes pretty carefully. I mean you'd have to predetermine what kind of a race you were going to drive: seven minutes of hard rock for charging at the start, then fifteen minutes of easy travelin' music for pacing yourself, a little Orange Blossom Special for puttin' the hammer down again, a soft guitar interlude for runnin' under the yellow and then eighteen seconds of frantic harpsichord music for a pit stop."

Mosley laughs. "It'd be like having music for the movie."

"If we really got civilized, you'd have air conditioning, automatic transmissions and cruise control."

"Next you'll want TV." Mosley's laughter is a soft Woody Woodpecker laugh with no hard edges.

"Maybe even remote cameras so you can watch the race you're driving from any one of a dozen points of view, from the first turn, from the Goodyear blimp, maybe even from inside the car."

We end up with thirty-three drivers driving the race in a penny arcade with a preprogrammed track and traffic pattern on a continuous roll, over which they guide their miniature cars. "Or we'll have slots in the track," Mosley caps it off, "and we'll just be passengers in the cars while somebody back in the tower is pushing the buttons."

129

Clifford Haverson, who works as a mechanic for Dan Gurney's team, brings up the latest antics of A. J. Foyt, who was fined twenty-five dollars for refusing to wear his Nomex underwear, got mad about that and skipped the drivers' meeting, winning himself another hundred-dollar fine. "It's just a popcorn meeting," Foyt said, "just a lot of bull we've heard before. I've been arguing with them all month, and I don't want to argue anymore."

"Why don't you ever do anything like that?" Clifford asks, "You're just always Mike Mosley, nice-guy race driver."

Mosley smiles.

"I can see the headlines when you win it: Unidentified Driver Wins 500."

Mosley laughs again, and it's infectious.

"I could hover over the track in a helicopter," Clifford mimes, "and pull you out of the car as you take the checkered flag. Then we could go somewhere and watch the search for you on television."

"That'd be great." Mosley seems delighted, as much by the idea of the monumental prank as by the idea of winning, and the smile behind his steel-rimmed aviator's glasses is almost more than his face can contain.

Hey, Mike, you're gonna win."

"Go get 'em!"

"Hey Bobby!"

I've never seen a 500 Festival Parade through downtown Indianapolis. I still haven't, but I'm watching something better: the faces of the people who are watching the parade, four hundred thousand of them, the organizers claim. Whatever their number, the spectators are a great parade themselves. Mike Mosley has asked me to ride with him in his pace car, one of thirty-three identically painted Buicks, one for each of the drivers. Each car has a sun roof so that the race drivers can sit on the roofs and wave to the crowd. I'm in the back seat of the car, peering through the windows at all the people who are looking at Mike and at Bobby Unser and Boom-Boom Cannon, who are riding atop the cars on either side of us. I feel as if I were a rare fish in an aquarium looking back at the multitudes streaming past my tank.

Following the formal drivers' meeting, the drivers, their families and guests have ridden from the Speedway to the parade marshaling area by the Indianapolis National Guard Armory in two police-escorted buses. Spirits on our bus were pretty high, the race drivers egging the bus driver on as he speeds in his cocoon of sirens, weaving intricately through the halted traffic. There's a surge of power and importance, the whole city stopped and waiting for us. "Of course," Johnny Rutherford says. "Without us they wouldn't have a show."

"I'm not so sure," I suggest. "I'll bet if they stopped running the race next year, almost all those people would come

Salt Walther being interviewed

anyway. It's a ritual as much as a race. They'd fill up those grandstands and the infield and make something happen."

"Maybe you're right." Rutherford smiles. "It'd probably go on for another three or four years anyway."

Dick Simon is wearing his hairpiece for the first time this month and whooping out rebel yells as people along Sixteenth Street stand and wave at the bus loads of celebrities.

Drinks are being served at the Armory before the parade, and as we go in to get a Coke, Mike and I pass Bob Hope and Tony Hulman coming out to take their places at the head of the parade. We walk through the corridors of the Armory, past the ominous rows of barred, cell-like doors to the reception room. It's crowded with familiar faces: those of the drivers of course, TV and movie stars, some of them familiar only from commercials. Barry Goldwater is shaking Mario Andretti's hand. Martin Milner wishes Mike good luck. Through the crowd I can see Phyllis Diller, Claude Akins and General Jimmy Doolittle.

Outside on the street, the bomb goes off to signal the start of the parade, and we hurry back to our cars. The streets are packed with people, standing, sitting on stools and lawn chairs, on balconies and bleachers, filling every visible window of every building, rooftops, and as we pass a six-story parking ramp, I

notice that standing room has been sold along the outside edge of each ramp so that it looks like a huge multilayer human sandwich. I notice an isolated niche high up on the war memorial, and there's a man standing in it, waving to the drivers below. It's a Roman mob scene worthy of Cecil B. De Mille.

As we move down the street, I forecast a pattern of those spectators who will root for Bobby Unser; seconds later, with amazing accuracy, my projection is borne out. "Hey Bobby!" I see their lips moving banging together twice, "Baa-Bee!" "The Indianapolis 500 festivities will be heard round the world on the world's largest radio network," I hear the parade announcer.

Near the end of the two-mile parade route, we pass a motor home in a parking lot. It faces the street and there's a loudspeaker on the roof. Behind the windshield, a woman holding a microphone. She's blushing. I can see even through the tinted windshield that her rather porcine features are flushed with a wide-eyed manic smile. She's thrilled, having the volume of the speaker at her command, but she doesn't know what to do with it. "Halooo." Her voice takes on the quality of a siren, and her excitement is hyped by the sound of her own voice. "Wooo, Wahooo." Now she's bouncing up and down on the driver's seat; her blond curls dangling like flaccid springs. The microphone has control of her, and she's about to go into orbit. "Halooo. WoooWeee." As the sound of her screaming fades behind us, I imagine her being dragged off to a rest home, driven totally insane by the sight of Bobby Unser and the self-perpetuating narcissism of the sound of her own voice.

Back at the Speedway, people are lined up for a quarter mile to get into the museum and to take a bus ride around the track. The sky is overcast, but nobody wants to talk about the possibility of rain for tomorrow. In Indianapolis, that just isn't done. The race has been halted by rain two of the past three years, and nobody can bear the thought that it might happen again—or worse, that it might be delayed until or have to be restarted on Monday.

I'm walking back to the garage area from the publicity office where I've just picked up my race-day credentials, and I'm stopped by one of the Speedway's ancient traffic controllers. His cheeks are flushed with broken capillaries, and he interrupts a conversation with himself to speak to me: "Hey there buddy, I can't let you by without a pass." I hold up my badge, and he nods in recognition of it. "Oh, okay. I had to yell at a fella this morning about keeping off the grass." He puts his hand on my forearm as a gesture of good will but, more significantly, to make sure I'll stick around to hear his story: "And this young cop comes up to me and says, 'You know who that is you was yellin' at?' 'Well no I don't,' I said. 'I just thought it was some guy walkin' on the grass.' 'Well, he's the governor of Arizona,' the cop says. 'Hell, it don't matter to me,' I tell him.

"Most people are pretty nice though." He laughs. "I had a

Photographers and reporters accompany Johnny Rutherford on his walk to Victory Lane

young fella come by this morning, and I told him to get off the grass. 'Look, you old wino,' he says to me, 'you can't tell me what to do.' 'Well, you look here young man,' I says to him. 'I'm a beer drinker and a lover.' 'Okay, yessir,' he says to me, and he gets right off right off the grass.''

He mumbles something to himself, lifts his Speedway baseball cap and wipes his forehead with the back of his hand. I'm about to walk on, but he stops me again. "I had a guy came by here this afternoon and he says, 'Will you guarantee if I walk down here on the pavement like you say that I won't get hit by a car?' 'Hell,' I tell him, 'I won't guarantee you won't get hit if you're walking inside that building.''' He gestures toward the museum. "'I won't guarantee you won't get hit by lightning.'''

"You're right," I say to him as I shake his hand, "no guarantees." He smiles, gives me a quick salute and goes on, telling stories to himself, as I continue on my way back to Gasoline Alley.

The difficult thing about trying to talk with a driver before the start of a race, especially this race, is that there's nothing to say. I'm standing on the track with Mike Mosley. We are leaning against the pit wall, facing the fourth row of cars, the row in which he will start from the middle position. The bands have passed, and the celebrities, and now there are only drivers, crews, officials and photographers on the track, about a thousand of them nervously milling around to kill the fifteen minutes before Tony Hulman will tell them to start their engines. Everyone seems a little zapped by all the pageantry and perhaps simply by the presence of another estimated 399,999 people. It's hard to realize that in a few minutes this piece of asphalt on which we're standing will be crowded with cars traveling 220 miles an hour. Perhaps foolishly, in an attempt to focus this moment, I make a stab at conversation. "Well, when it gets to this point," I say, "it must seem just like a race."

"Yeah," Mosley nods philosophically, "it looks like it's going to happen, so there's no point in worrying about it."

A man with a tape recorder comes out of the crowd, thrusts a microphone in front of Mike's mouth and makes my lame attempt at communication seem almost profound. "Mike, what's your race plan? Can you talk about it?"

I imagine Mike saying, "Yeah, if I can just keep from throwing up all over your microphone." At this point the tension is so high I can feel it resonating through my legs and up my back. I'm as nervous as I've ever been before driving a race, and here I'm only a spectator. But Mike keeps it together and deals with this inane question as straightforwardly as he would have if it had been asked two weeks earlier: "We're just gonna try and get through the first few laps and then drive as hard a race as we can."

"You've got a pretty good car this year, don't you?"

Rutherford steps out of car after race called, the first man to walk to the winner's circle

A. J. Foyt, distraught after the rain ended
his chance for a fourth 500 victory

"Well, we'd like to have a little more power. I just hope it can run all day."

"What would it mean to you to win this one Mike?" *Jesus,* I'm thinking, *this guy doesn't quit.*

"It'd be..." Mike tries to find an intelligent answer to this obvious question, then shrugs his shoulders. "It'd be great."

Now it's time for the drivers to get in their cars. I shake Mike's hand. "I'll see you..."

"Wherever." He smiles.

I run to the front of the starting field. An overly ardent singer with a group of hyperactive dancing children who all look like they've stepped out of a toothpaste commercial is melodramatizing the national anthem to the point of sedition. I wince at each high vibrato, hoping he'll swallow his uvula and spare my ears. I'm trying to get a photograph of Tony Hulman as he speaks *those immortal words*, but he's lost in a forest of microphones. Jim Nabors again drawls through "Back Home Again in Indiana," a barrage of red, then white, then blue balloons is released against the now darkly threatening sky. Tony Hulman speaks, the starters grind, engines begin revving and I'm sprinting to take up my camera position on the inside of the first turn.

I'm thinking about Billy Scott in his first Indy start as the field passes on the parade lap. When I talked with him earlier in the morning, he was thrilled by the pageantry, as if it were all in celebration of his having made the race. He seemed excited rather than nervous, more as if he were going to ride in a parade than be caught up in the sweep of 24,000 HP. Mosley is late getting started and hurries past to catch up with his place in the formation. The field passes again, faster this time, the cars snaking violently to heat up their tires, and the track announcer's voice follows them around. *Down the back straight...taking their positions through turn three...looking good in the north chute...into turn four now, the pace car dropping down, pulling into the pit lane, Johnny Rutherford now in control, bringing them toward the start, in good formation, keeping their interval, AND THEY'VE GOT THE GREEN.* The low roar of the engines glissades to a scream, the air is saturated with the vapor of methanol fumes, and I can feel the vibrations in the grass beneath my feet and against the exposed skin of my arms. *And the Sixtieth running of the Indianapolis Five Hundred is under way, the greatest spectacle in racing.* The cars disappear into the short chute and a dozen bombs explode in the air in rapid succession. I'm startled and wince, momentarily mistaking them as reports from a horrendous crash. I hear an enormous cheer from the hordes in the snake pit behind me and from the grandstands across the track, so many voices that I can hear them resonate over the scream of the cars. I've completely lost myself. The excitement blurs my vision; and all I see is a chain of bright colors.

There are a few moments of silence, and I can hear a cricket somewhere in the grass between me and the track. I can hear the roar building again as the cars zoom back down the front straight, and I imagine what the drivers are seeing, the wings and tires ahead of them, blurred by vibrations and by the dust and smoke, dodging and darting, testing for an opening to pass. The first cars blast past me again and the roar becomes a scream again, raw from their exhausts. This time I get control of myself

and begin sorting them out, Rutherford in the lead, followed by Johncock, Sneva and Foyt. On the third lap, Foyt is on Rutherford's tail. On the fourth lap, just in front of me, Foyt passes Rutherford. But there are no gaps. The whole field is close. Rutherford and Foyt will dice like this, swapping the lead between pit stops, throughout the next 250 miles. I see Mosley trying to pass in the short chute, but he seems to lack the power to get by the car ahead of him. He goes high on the outside, then is forced to drop back to set up for the second turn.

Thirty-five laps have gone by, and the field is running under the yellow. There's a moment of silence; the first turn is empty. Then the spectators in the stands across the track rise in a wave as the green light comes on. They can see what's coming down the main straight. Ten cars pass, nose to tail. There's another brief moment of silence in their wake, and I can hear ten thousand excited conversations like ten thousand fragments of falling glass, as they settle back in their seats. Then their voices are blanketed by another wave of four cars.

At 91 laps, Mike Mosley coasts in, out of fuel. His crew runs down the pit lane to meet him and pushes him to his pit. I'm standing in the press room, watching the race on a TV monitor; it's the one way I can see what's happening all around the track. I feel the wall behind me vibrate as the cars dive into the first turn. At 101 laps, the rain starts falling and the race is stopped. Rain is getting to be part of the Indy tradition; it has stopped the race three of the last four years. This time it passes, and a parade of pace cars and crash trucks and an absurd-looking jet-powered blower circles the track to dry it out for the restart. The race cars pull into the pits and a curiously relaxed half-time atmosphere prevails. There's nothing to do now but wait.

I find Billy Scott sitting on the pit wall by his car. I sit next to him and ask how he dropped so suddenly from sixteenth to twenty-third.

"I had a loose wheel," he says. "I went into turn one, and it wouldn't turn. I went way up in the gray. I looked at my left wheel, and it was turning, but the right one was just going *oooha, oooha, oooha.*" He wiggles his hand as if imitating a fish. "Then I went into turn two and it went *oooha, oooha, oooha.*"

"And then you went *oooha, oooha, oooha,*" I suggest.

"Yeah," he laughs, "at least I was sure something wasn't right."

"Either that or you forgot something important about this track."

"Yeah, really." He laughs again.

"Well, have a great second half," I tell him as I get up to go.

"Thanks coach," he says. "We gotta drive this one harder. That wheel mighta cost me Rookie of the Year."

I stop by Foyt's pit and hear him explaining to a group of newsmen how Johnny Rutherford had picked up twenty seconds on him under the yellow.

"Did he do anything you wouldn't have done?" one of them asks.

A. J. hesitates a moment, then smiles weakly. "No, I guess not really," he says and turns back toward his crew.

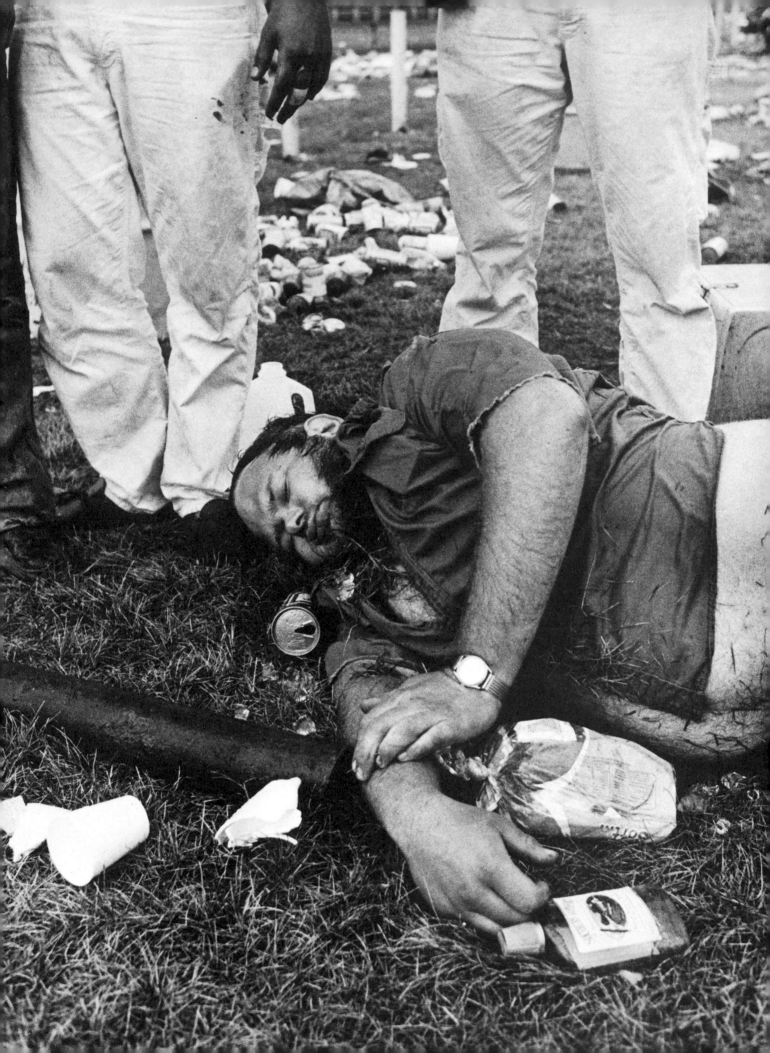

At three o'clock the track is judged dry enough for a restart, and the cars are lined up single file in the pit lane. While the drivers get strapped in, I hurry back out to my spot inside the first turn. At three-ten it starts raining again. The crews cover the cars and drivers with tarps and sheets of plastic, and everyone who can runs for cover. At three-twenty the race is called in one of the most anticlimactic finishes in its sixty-year history. Johnny Rutherford is declared the winner of the Indianapolis 255, beating out Foyt by 3.7 seconds, and is the first driver in the history of the race to walk, rather than drive to Victory Lane. Foyt is furious and distraught, foiled again by the weather. For the past nine years he's been trying to become the first man to win the 500 four times. In his frustration, he threatens to file a protest, but eventually realizes it would be futile. There's no recourse against the rain.

The party is suddenly over, and everything is confusion. The multitudes in the infield have run for their cars or broken out sheets of transparent plastic to cover themselves and their drowned picnics. They will sit and steam for hours as the greatest spectacle in traffic congestion tries to sort itself out. I'm in no hurry to join the crush, and will let it ease up before I drive back to my motel.

I stop by Mike Mosley's garage and have a beer. The car sits outside under a tarp, and a party is going on in the one-stall garage. Running out of fuel had dropped Mike back to sixteenth place. He has his driving suit half off, folded down around his waist, but has given up the idea of changing in this crowd. It's raining harder now, really pouring. Everyone, except perhaps Rutherford, would have liked to have seen the race restarted and run to its conclusion, but they are, nevertheless, relieved that it's over.

Clifford Haverson has joined the party. He tells Mike how Vern Schuppan, Dan Gurney's Australian rookie driver, said to Gurney during a pit stop, "I think I'm getting the hang of this. This is fun," then went back out and improved his speed markedly.

"Boy, he's really a nice guy," Clifford says earnestly.

"Yeah, he is." Mosley nods in agreement.

"Really easygoing and..." Clifford looks at Mike, they break into laughter and complete the thought simultaneously, "and dumb."

"Yeah," Mosley is still laughing, "anybody who thinks that's fun out there is dumb. It's just scary, that's what it is." I'm delighted with his frankness, and we all laugh again with relief.

I stop by Billy Scott's garage to say good-by. Everyone is crowded in around his beautiful red, white and blue car. They all seem happy, especially Billy's mother. His loose wheel cost him seven places and the Rookie of the Year Award he'd been working toward all month. "But that's racing," he says, shrugging his shoulders. He knows he's run well and has the experience of one Indy behind him. "I hope I see ya before next year," he says as we shake hands. "Give me a call when you get to California."

EPILOGUE

Our revels are now ended. These our actors
As I fortold you, were all spirits and
Are melted into air, into thin air...

How could I be so naive? The race had seemed to fade so insignificantly in the downpour that it had taken on a dreamlike quality. It was almost as if it had been a rather pointless fantasy we had constructed in the rain, there in Mike Mosley's garage. No one could take issue with the weather. It played out its pattern, as totally indifferent to the greatest spectacle in racing, to this mid-American celebration of the rites of spring, as if it had drowned out a pastoral tryst or a sandlot baseball game. And because the race had been so arbitrarily terminated, did I assume that the multitudes had likewise been dissolved? What did I think was going to happen to those 400,000 people?

In past years, the postrace traffic has been merely a stream to be crossed on my ten-minute walk back to the Speedway Motel. But this year I am staying at a Ramada Inn, a short three miles away. I have killed an hour and a half following the race and figure that, by now, it will be a moderate, if perhaps mildly circuitous drive back to a hot shower and some dry clothes. I know I'll have to follow the traffic pattern east on Sixteenth Street until I can catch a left to Thirty-eighth, turn left again and cruise to the door of my room. I pull out of the garage area parking lot, get into the flow, through the tunnel and out of the Speedway with no delays. *All I'll need is a little patience*, I tell myself. I flick on the radio. "I know it may seem like they're sending you to nowhere," the voice oozes, "but the police really have your best interests in mind. So follow their instructions and they'll direct you as quickly and safely as possible to your destination." The traffic is six lanes one way, like water running out of a bathtub, 400,000 half-drowned lives funneling out into America.

A mile or so down Sixteenth Street, I catch a left through a residential area. This street takes me to Lafayette, which my map tells me will intersect with Thirty-eighth, and it does. It's been twenty minutes, and I'm cruising down Thirty-eighth Street, three blocks from my motel. The traffic's heavy, but I'm home-free. But wait! Two cars ahead of me, a police car is pulling across all three lanes of traffic. He's stopping us, making us U-turn and go back the other way. Now I am lost, on a freeway to No-Name Creek. I take the first exit, head north and begin an hour-and-a-half search for a safe route to the Indies. It's pouring again now. I find a freeway that will take me right to my motel, but there's no southbound entrance ramp, anywhere. I turn back and search, circumnavigating accidents, circling defensively to find a weak spot in the outbound flow. Finally I see a police car parked on the shoulder. I pull up behind him, get out into the deluge and knock on his window. "I need help." My voice is on the edge of cracking.

"It's easy," he says. "Just take a left here, go two miles to the light, turn right, and you'll be on Thirty-eighth, real close to where you're going."

"Thank you sir." I feel an impulse to kiss him.

Now I'm coming up on the light. I make the right turn on